The
Beekay Guide
to
Carp Rigs

Kevin Maddocks and Julian Cundiff

First published in 1996 by Beekay International.
Reprinted 1997, 1998, 2000, 2002.
This edition published by
Coch-y-bonddu Books, Machynlleth. March 2005.

ISBN 978 1 904 78404 3

Published & distributed by
COCH-Y-BONDDU BOOKS
MACHYNLLETH, POWYS, SY20 8DJ
Tel 01654 702837   Fax 01654 702857
www.anglebooks.com

Printed in Great Britain by
CPI Antony Rowe, Chippenham, Wiltshire

Contents

Drawings by Brian Atkins

Introduction

If a carp angler of 30 years ago had been told that a whole book would be devoted to describing 'rigs' for carp fishing, he would have found it hard to believe: tie a hook on your line, he would probably have said, and this is the only rig you would need!

Even today, some carp anglers might query the need for a book of this kind, but experience has shown us that a knowledge of the many different set-ups which ingenious anglers have devised to deceive carp is essential for success in most waters.

It would be a mistake to credit carp with intelligence or the ability to reason, but of all fish they do have the greatest aptitude for learning by experience. The intensive fishing pressure in many carp waters today - especially those which contain big fish - has resulted in the carp being caught with some frequency. This inevitably results in the fish that are often hooked and caught becoming very wary of baits, and their remarkably sensitive mouths and protractile lips can detect anything unnatural about food presented to them by anglers.

If you've ever watched surface feeding carp rejecting, again and again, a piece of crust or mini-floater with a hook and line attached, you will have some idea of the way they inspect baits you can't see, such as those presented of the bottom.

Anglers, however, can eventually out-think fish, and over the past 20 years have developed many different methods of deceiving wary carp into thinking that their baits are natural.

In this book, every sensible rig and method for modern carp fishing is described and illustrated in detail. Any angler who wants to catch more carp cannot fail to improve his success rate by reading this book, and by using the methods described. There have been rig books before, but none which are as comprehensive and which contain as much information as there is in our book. Take it with you when you go fishing, and you will be ready for almost any presentation problem which may arise.

We can justly claim to be two of the country's most successful captors of carp, many of which have come from a great variety of waters, and with this book we bring you precise information on every known successful carp rig ever invented; not only this, but our lengthy and carefully researched work shows you how and where to use the rigs and even the baits and methods to go with the rigs. Previous books have been brief and much less comprehensive than ours; the rigs and methods in it have been tried and tested by both of us in some of the hardest waters in Europe.

Today, all anglers have access to excellent tackle and baits, and there are so many carp waters, many of which are club and day ticket, that anyone can fish good waters containing very large carp. It has been proved, beyond doubt, that often the main difference between the average anglers, and those who get the best carp catches, is a knowledge of modern rigs and how to use them.

After the publication of this book, there is no reason why anyone who reads it and learns to use the rigs listed in the correct situations should not be as successful as the leading carp anglers in the country.

We have kept no secrets, and we hope that everyone who buys this book will find a dramatic increase in their catches; if this is so, we shall have succeeded in our intention of informing every carp angler in this country the way to success in modern carp fishing.

Kevin Maddocks and Julian Cundiff.

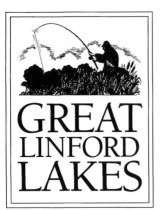

1. The Carp and Outside Influences

Many people who pick up this book on carp rigs will expect it to be full of illustrations and technical jargon on hooks, leads, hooklengths and the like as that's what it's all about, surely? Not so! To decide which rig to use it is essential to have a basic understanding of the carp and its feeding habits and how outside influences can have an effect on which rig you should choose. For that reason this chapter will contain advice on those factors, so helping you make the right choice, or make the right rig even more effective. Don't just jump past this information and look for something more radical, you may well miss out on the essentials!

THE CARP - A LESSON IN BIOLOGY

Whilst we all should know it, it's easy to forget that carp are very different from humans and how we perceive, find and take in food is different from how a carp will (Fig. 1). Remember that the next time you drag a line aligner across your hand or taste a boily to see if it tastes nice! Got the picture? So to start with let's look at how a carp breathes and feeds.

RESPIRATION

The carp takes oxygen from the water through its gills in order to breathe. The gills are situated just behind the head of the fish and are protected by plates of bone called gill covers. To breathe the carp will take water into its mouth with its gill covers closed. The mouth is then closed, the gill covers are opened and the floor of its mouth is raised so forcing water out of the gills. To ensure no water is pushed out through the lips, the carp has a thin flap of skin hanging from the roof of the mouth (sometimes referred to by carp anglers as the "curtain") which creates a seal and ensures that the complete flow passes through the gills. Sadly, some carp no longer have this flap because of damage caused by regular hooking! Because the gills are fine blood vessels, oxygen is passed through the outer membrane and into the bloodstream so completing the process. Carp require certain amounts of oxygen to survive and in order to decide where to fish and with which rig, it's necessary to know where oxygenated water can be best found at certain

1

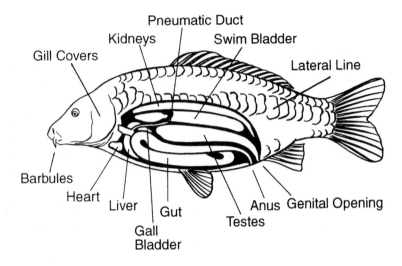

Fig. 1. Carp's vital organs

times of the year. In the summer in the shallows the water will be warmer and will have less dissolved oxygen. So even if the carp are in the shallows they may be disinclined to feed, no matter what kind of rig you use. Also, at certain times the weedbeds will be taking oxygen out of the water and replacing it with carbon dioxide, especially during the hours of darkness and at first light, which compounds the problem. So "rig shy" carp may well be oxygen depleted carp!

SENSES AS AIDS TO FEEDING

Carp have a similar sensory system to humans in that they are able to hear, touch, taste and smell items around them. This has great importance when deciding which rig to use and how its components may put the carp on its guard as it considers the hookbait. The senses of a carp are hearing - taste - smell - sight and touch.

a) Hearing - although carp do not have ears as humans have, they can hear much more acutely than we can. The carp "hears" by detecting sound waves passing through the water. These sound waves are converted into messages in the carp's brain and are translated into noise. The carp's hearing is particularly sensitive and the tiny bones in their ears called ossicles can detect and amplify the smallest of sound waves passing through water. So although the splash of a rig entering the water may well attract the carp, the carp may identify this with danger eventually and treat the area with suspicion.

b) Taste/Smell - these two senses are to be grouped together as they make up the carp's olfactory sense. Carp can taste and smell items in the water and can do this in a number of ways. Nostrils near the eyes of the carp allow water to enter and the highly sensitive olfactory system can then pick up any substances which have been dissolved into that water. The carp will then identify this as a viable food source or not. When a carp takes in a potential food item into the mouth the lining of the mouth which contains chemically sensitive cells will send a message to the carp's brain as to whether that food item is a viable food source. If this is so, the carp may then will continue to feed until satisfied. However, if the carp decides that the item is not a food item it will reject the item taken in and may bolt from the area. Although carp will take in many items as potential food items, they have the ability to reject them!

c) Sight - carp have the ability to see through the eyes situated on either side of the head. Unlike humans who have a straight line of vision, carp see out of the water sideways and upwards at an angle of around 49° through each eye. Anything outside of this angle out of the water will be invisible to the carp. In water the carp's vision will be extremely limited in certain cases and extremely effective in other cases. If the water is deep, clouded, murky, full of suspended silt particles, the carp's vision will be negligible. Clearly this is even less when light is at a minimum. However, in shallow, clear water with bright sun the carp's ability to see items will improve. Be aware of this when using crude or obvious end tackles and presentations in such circumstances!

d) Touch - the tactile sense of touch in a carp is utilised in two ways. In the standard form of direct touch where a carp comes across and brushes/takes in a presentation it can feel that it has done so. Nerve fibres in the carp's skin send messages to its brain and if the carp does not identify the item touched as a viable food item it will reject it and may spook from the area. Secondly, the carp has an ability to sense touch through its lateral line. The lateral line on a carp which runs from its head to its tail is comprised of fine fluid filled tubes which open to the outside by tiny pores. Similar to hairs they can detect very slight movements in the water which assist them when locating potential food sources or detecting items to avoid. Carp can also "touch" potential food items with their barbules which are located either side of the mouth. Once a carp has located a food item it can use the barbules to touch the food source. It may well not be able to see the item with its eyes but it can assess it with its barbules just as well, if not better. The carp may well decide to take the food item in or may decide to reject it if that food item is attached to a carp rig!

So what does all that tell us when all we are trying to do is to decide which rig to use? Simple! No matter how attractive your food item may be, to enter the carp's mouth and to hopefully hook the carp it must pass the

A winter $32\frac{1}{2}$ from Withy Pool caught whilst field testing Kesmark's
Combi-Splice hooklength material.

An Amnesia 'D' rig accounted for this fabulous fish.

sensory test. Crude end tackles and presentations may be visually unacceptable and when touched may be rejected immediately. Carp are not stupid and will use their own senses for survival and survival means avoiding the obvious and dangerous.

HOW CARP FEED?

Having seen how the carp's senses greatly influence how it feeds we shall now look at how the carp takes in food items. No matter what rig you use, in order to hook and land a carp by fair means the hook has to enter the carp's mouth. Yes, occasionally an item will enter the carp's mouth accidentally but most enter the mouth when the carp takes in an item to assess its value as a food item. Having "sensed" a potential food item, the carp will seek to evaluate it via direct contact inside the mouth. To draw in that item of food the carp usually takes it in as it would take in water to convert the oxygen contained within it. The mouth's opened, the gill covers close and water is drawn into the mouth. Anything contained in the water which is drawn into the mouth will enter that area likewise. The mouth is closed, the floor of the mouth is raised and the gill covers are opened. Excess water is driven out and the carp uses its tongue to hold in food items if they are evaluated in a positive way.

Clearly this sounds a very long winded process but in reality it's very quick indeed as anyone who has watched carp feeding will know. Because the carp has the ability to draw in and blow out items contained in the water this is called "sucking and blowing" and this is a common way of feeding found on many waters. Carp can suck in a large amount of water (obviously dependent on the size of the carp and its ability to generate a vacuum inside its mouth) and items up to eight inches away can be drawn in with that water. When the carp "blows out," items can be displaced over twelve inches, again dependent upon the size of the fish and density of the items in question. As well as sucking and blowing, carp also have the ability to pick items up in their lips. By extending their lips and using a very slight sucking movement, the food item is gently taken in. In effect this is a moderated/careful form of sucking and blowing and is not a completely dissimilar feeding style. The mouth of the carp is purely and simply a hole which allows food items to be taken in. Once inside the mouth, if not rejected, the teeth (identical to human's teeth but a little smaller) located in the throat and known as pharyngeal teeth will grind the food item against the roof of the mouth in order to break it down before passing it into the digestive system. Carp do not have a stomach as we do and food in the digestive system is broken down by gastric juices known as enzymes. Food, once broken down, is absorbed and used in the carp's body for survival.

Always remember that when you use a carp rig the hook has to enter the carp's mouth to hook it. Seek to make the hookbait as attractive as possible so that the carp wants to feed on it, make the rig one which allows the food item to be taken in rather than detected before entry and ensure that once in the carp's mouth if the carp seeks to reject it it is difficult to do so. That process of finding a rig which will satisfy all those criteria is known as choosing the right rig.

FACTORS AFFECTING THE CARP'S FEEDING

Unfortunately it's not possible to say with absolute certainty how a carp will feed on any given water and which rig to choose. The carp's feeding behaviour will be affected by many criteria and these are as follows:-

1. The personal characteristics of the carp - this would be its mouth shape, mouth size, body shape and so on. Carp are similar to human beings in that they have their own individual characteristics. Not all carp feed in ideal feeding conditions and not all carp stop feeding in poor feeding conditions. At times they may well be predictable but not in a way that anyone can predict with certainty how to outwit them.

2. Angler pressure - when carp have been caught time and time again on a particular type of rig or bait or even in a particular place in the lake, they may change their normal feeding habits to avoid being hooked. For the

Perfect bite indication was essential with this French 43
caught at 200 metres range.

purposes of this book it explains why certain rigs seem to "blow" when numbers of carp have been caught on one particular form of presentation. Carp seek to avoid this and may feed in such a way that the rig is not as effective as it used to be. You would then have to vary your rig to outwit the carp. Not only does angler pressure over many years come into play, it also has an effect when many anglers are fishing one water at the same time. An abundance of free offerings may well fill the carp up before they even encounter the hookbait. Numbers of lines across the lake may well spook or panic the carp, so making positive feeding unlikely. Recasting time and time again could panic the carp as they start to associate leads crashing through the water as a danger signal and so on.

3. Confidence in the food item - we will cover this in more detail in the chapter on hookbaits but it's vital that you recognise that confidence or otherwise in the hookbait is of paramount importance. If the carp is confident in that food item it may well take it in positively which can only increase the likelihood of hooking the carp. However, if the carp is wary or unsure of the food item, it may approach its feeding in a cautious manner no matter what rig the hookbait is presented on.

4. Time of year - whilst carp do feed all year round they do not feed with the same voracity all year round. If the carp are feeding strongly in the

summer months they may take in food items confidently, but in winter in less than ideal conditions feeding may be sporadic and cautious. Whilst you should always use the best rig possible, once feeding conditions are less than ideal it is an idea to ring the changes to try to outwit the cautious and wary feeders.

5. Barometric pressure - this has a great effect on the feeding of carp and the consequent effectiveness or otherwise of your rig. During high pressure weather, which is known as anti-cyclones (red hot still days, clear and colder nights) usually the carp will not feed as strongly no matter which rig you use to present your hookbait. With low pressure which is known as depressions (overcast skies, mild south-westerly winds, rain etc) the carp's feeding should increase due to increased oxygen levels, water turbulence and lower light levels. In such conditions a good rig should produce and if you are not receiving action you should look critically at your rig choice.

Of course, there are countless other outside influences which affect how carp feed, and which rig to use, but for the purposes of this book the advice given should assist you.

If the carp are confident in your bait, there is little angler pressure, feeding conditions are good, carp are in your swim and you are not getting takes, you will need to look very carefully at the rig you are using.

If the carp have not built up confidence in the bait, if feeding conditions are less than ideal, if angler pressure is extreme and you are not sure about where to locate the carp, don't automatically think your rig is to blame!

A rig will only catch carp if:-

a) it is where the carp are prepared to feed
b) it's there at the time they are prepared to feed
c) it has a hookbait on it that the carp are willing to take in.

DON'T ALWAYS BLAME THE RIG!

2. The Importance of Feature Finding

Having established the factors that influence how carp feed and how they can affect your choice of rig, the next considerations you have to be aware of are features and their effect on your choice of rig. Whether you fish a gravel pit or a weedy water, whether it's in a huge inland sea or a quiet farm pond, you should not decide which rig to use until you are sure of the nature of the lake bed you are fishing on. Although throughout this chapter we shall refer to "lake bed" it also relates to rivers, canals and so on. Do not cast out a rig until you've established what you are casting into or onto. A good bait on a good rig ceases to be of any real value if that rig is not suitable for the area it is cast to. You can copy all the latest rigs and baits from the latest publications but unless used correctly they may go to waste. So how do we decide which rig to use? This is by finding out about the nature of the bottom onto which we are casting and therein lies the importance of feature finding.

SURFACE FISHING AND FEATURE FINDING?

Generally when we talk of feature finding we are looking for features that are below the surface of the water such as gravel bars, silt pockets, plateaux and so on. However, when fishing on the surface for carp it's also vital to be aware of the features that will dictate which rig you should use. Luckily these features are usually visual so we can use our eyesight to come to a decision rather than having to resort to specialist leading and plumbing techniques. Look at the water out in front of you. Is it open water allowing you to use fine floater presentations or are you fishing near weed and snags which means you will have to strengthen/change your rig? Are there any subsurface features which you need to be aware of when deciding which floater rig to use? Eyesight is a start but don't forget the usefulness of polaroid glasses, binoculars and suchlike. Things are not always as they first appear.

STANDARD FISHING AND FEATURE FINDING?

Make no mistake about it, you cannot decide which rig to use until you are sure of the nature of the bottom you are fishing on or over. Without knowing whether you are fishing on silt, weed, gravel and suchlike it's impossible to pick the correct rig. Unfortunately, because many features are subsurface you will not always be able to see them with your eyes and you need to plumb and lead the water to find the nature of its topography. Even if you've been given advice on what is out in front of you, it's vital that you verify it for yourself. Of course, advice is a good pointer to locating the carp but to decide on which rig to use you need to plumb and lead the water thoroughly. Even if a feature is visual such as a weedbed, snag, island etc, you still need to plumb and lead around that feature to find out what you are casting your lead and hookbait to. You need to be aware of what is subsurface and how it will affect your rig choice.

FEATURE FINDING

There are two main ways to locate features which are subsurface, these are by "plumbing" and "leading". Both complement each other and on many waters to choose the right rig you need to have both plumbed the water and leaded it.

Plumbing - the use of a marker float to ascertain the depth of water you are casting into. Leading - the use of a lead to feel the nature of the lake bed upon which you are casting.

PLUMBING THE WATER

For all intents and purposes waters will fall into one of two categories; those with weed and those which are clear, although many waters have both! Where weed is a problem you have to plumb using one particular kind of set-up. If it's weed free you can use another set-up.

a) Plumbing in open water - where the water in front of you is weed free, such as in some gravel pits, silty ponds etc, you can use the set-up as illustrated (Fig. 2). Although its use may be fairly self explanatory this is how to use it correctly. The marker float is attached directly to the mainline with a link clip. This is then attached to a swivel which acts as a stopper for the large swivel attached to the lead. Next to the swivel is a large rubber shockbead and next to that is a large eyed swivel which is clipped to the lead. You need to use a large swivel to allow the line to run smoothly through it when you are paying off line. Pick your aiming point and cast directly at it. Once the lead hits the water and the line sinks, wind down until the float is tight to the lead. When your line is tight, open your bale arm whilst holding the line in the other hand. Start to pay off line, about twelve inches (30cm) at a time until the float reaches the surface. Once it does reach the surface count the number of pay-offs to give you the depth of the water in feet (30cm). If necessary, record the information on a map or plan of the water, wind in a couple

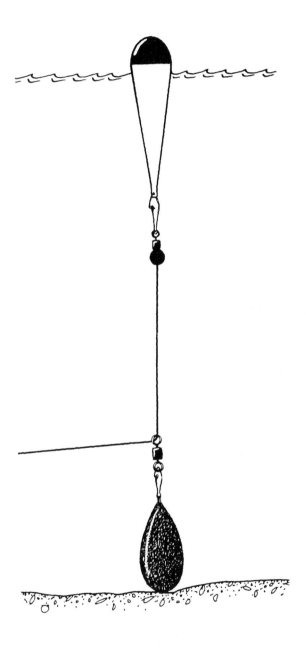

Fig. 2. Open water plumbing set-up

LEAD PERFECTION
by
KORDA DEVELOPMENTS

Korda specialise soley in the manufacture of quality carp leads. Like any specialist w
have become very experienced at what we do. We have used this experience to enhan
our designs to achieve the most technically perfect range of leads ever made.

We are very proud to present to you
KORDA FLATLINERS

LESS TANGLES - Both designs are tapered at the back of the lead to avoid tangling.
CARP FRIENDLY - Unique hard casing surrounds buried swivel to prevent tethering.
IMPROVED HOOKING - Buried swivel and flat sides maximise bolt effect.

FLATLINER DISTANCE

We have maximised stability in flight to enchance distance. Four flat sides improve hooking without reducing distance. Available in 1½oz, 2oz, 2½oz, 3oz, 3½oz, 4oz.

FLATLINER PEAR

Dumpy shape plus two f sides maximise contact w the lake bed thus maximisi bolt effect. Ideal for the mc difficult waters.
Available in 1½oz, 2c 2½oz, 3oz, 3½oz, 4oz.

KORDA SWIVEL LEADS

LESS TANGLES - Both are neatly tapered towards swivel area to minimize tangles.
STRONGER HELICOPTER RIGS - Round eye Berkley swivels maximise knot strength.
SENSITIVE RUNNING RIGS - Large round eye swivel minimises friction on line.

PEAR LEAD

Dumpy shape gives a more instant bolt effect. Ideal for short to medium range work. Available in 1½oz, 2oz, 2½oz, 3oz, 3½oz, 4oz.

DISTANCE LEAD

Unique weight forward desi with a bullet nose keeps t Lead totally stable in flig improving accuracy a adding distance. We a confident this lead will ca further than any other lead the market. Available in 1½ 2oz, 2½oz, 3oz, 3½oz, 4 4½oz

 CAMOU COATED - All designs now available with durable plastic coating low visibility Weedy Green and Muddy Brown.

NEW **KORDA RIG BOOK** - Tons of information on leads and rigs professional F drawing plus definitive guest articles by Cundiff, Paisley, Maylin, Bojk Gibbinson, Jackson, Kavangh, Clarke...UNBELIEVABLE!!!!

Korda Leads are available from all leading Tackle Shops.
Trade enquiries welcome
8A ELM PARADE, ELM PARK, ESSEX, RM12 4QG *or phone* 0802 2537

of yards (2 metres) and repeat the sequence. This will give you the depth at this new spot. Once you've marked out the depths along one sightline, cast a little to the left or right and continue the procedure until you have an accurate recording of the depths in front of you (Fig. 3). Using a plumbing method like this will show you the depth of water in front of you and at what distance out those depths are. Whilst some people may argue that it's not depth that's important but the nature of the lake bed, that is incorrect. By knowing the exact depth and location of drop offs and plateaux you will be able to decide which rig to use. Plumbing clear waters properly is essential if you are to make the right rig choice.

b) Plumbing in weed - when you have bottom weed in your swim you need to use a different kind of set up (Fig. 4). Because bottom weed would clog even a large eyed swivel you have to use this alternative set-up. Furthest away from the reel is a large lead and that is tied to a twelve inch (30cm) piece of heavy braid. Attached to the other end of the braid is a swivel. This braid is the length which goes into the bottom weed and, because it keeps the float at least twelve inches (30cm) from the lead, the float should not get caught up in the weed. That swivel is tied to the mainline which has a large rubber bead, a large marker float with line through the middle of it, a second small bead and a stop knot. Cast

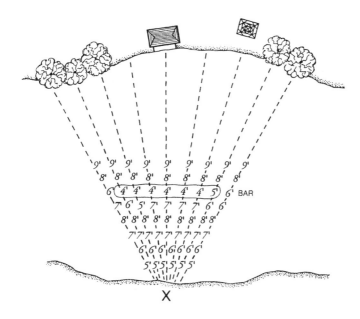

Fig. 3. Map out the area in front of you

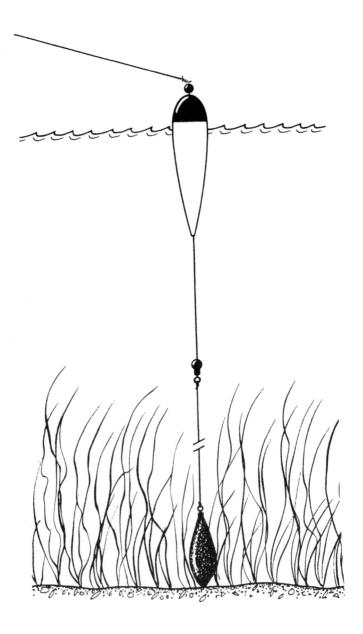

Fig. 4. Weedy water plumbing set-up

Brenda Maddocks caught this upper 30 on a pop-up two metres off the bottom when no other carp anglers could catch!

In conditions like these, the rig needs to be spot-on!

your float at the required distance in the required line when it is set to
what you think is the depth at that point. If the float does not show you
have set it too shallow and you will need to move the stop knot towards
you to increase the depth. If the float stays on its side on the surface and
your line is slack, your float is set too deep and your stop knot will have
to be moved towards the lead to decrease the depth. Obviously, to do this
you have to wind in each and every time. When your float is at the correct depth it will sit proud in the water. Wind in, record the depth and do
it again, and again, and again ... As with plumbing in clear waters, it is
vital to know the depth of water in front of you even if you think visual
weedbeds make it obvious where to cast to. Often weed grows on either
side of bars and plateaux and it's only through accurate plumbing that
you can locate the precise areas to cast your chosen rig to.

LEADING THE WATER

Whilst it's vital to know the depth of water you are fishing in, it's just as
important to know exactly what you are fishing in or on. The only way to
do this is by a technique called "leading the water" and was first written
about in Carp Fever. It entails dragging a lead over the lake bed to see if
the vibrations transmitted down the line can tell you a little about the
nature of the lake bed you are fishing on. If you've never done this before

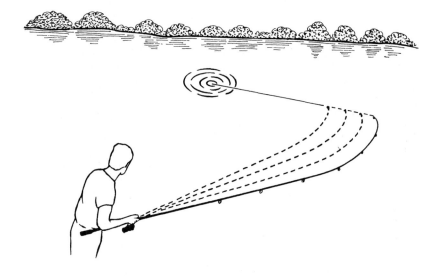

Fig. 5. Leading the water

it all sounds complicated, but be assured it's not. Practise the following technique and in time you will be able to distinguish silt from silkweed, snags from gravel bars and so on.

To lead the water all you need to do is tie a large lead to your mainline, or even use an unbaited end tackle, and cast it out to the area you intend to fish. By standing sideways to the water, and moving your rod in an arc, your line will tighten; move the lead and the nature of the lake's bed will be transmitted down the line into your hands (Fig. 5). Various features feel different and give their own tell-tale plucks, knocks and tightenings of the line. In time you will be able to tell what your lead has landed on and is being pulled through. At first this is a little difficult, but with experience you should come to grips with it. Always use a large weight to pick up the features and don't use too sloppy a rod or you will lose the feel of the features.

To aid you as to how certain features show up when a lead is dragged across them we've included a list of the major ones and how your lead, line and rod tip will respond.

BOTTOM WEED

Your lead will be a bit difficult to move at first and will keep plucking as it pulls through the weed. When you bring the lead in, strands may be caught around it.

Heavy weed and fishing at range – the worst case scenario; 25.12!!

THICK WEED

Your lead will feel solidly embedded and will be almost immovable. Your rod tip will bend right round and your line will feel like it is attached to a dead weight. You may have to point the rod at the lead to draw it in.

SNAGS

Your lead will be coming in but will then stop suddenly with the rod tip banging right round. Your lead will jar against the snag and, if it is a particularly bad one, you may have to pull for a break.

GRAVEL

Patches of gravel will feel like you are running your knuckles over billiard balls. You will feel the tremors through your line and your rod tip will keep flicking back and forward. Larger pieces of gravel and stones will give your rod tip an even more pronounced kick or knock.

PULLING UP GRAVEL BARS

Your line will start to tighten and your rod tip will bend round gently as the lead moves up the slope of the bar.

ON TOP OF THE BAR

Your line will still be fairly tight but your rod tip will start to move back to its original shape.

PULLING OFF THE BAR

Your line will go slack and your rod tip will flick back as if a fish has just dropped off. Your lead will have just fallen down the side of the bar. The more slack line you have to wind in, the higher the bar is in the water and the steeper its sides are.

SILT

Your lead will feel as though it's being pulled through cotton wool and, although there are no kicks on the rod tip, it feels as though you have extra weight on your lead. It will feel hard to pull out of and then smooth on a steady draw-back.

CLEAR SPOTS IN WEED

After a period of plucking, the rod tip will flick straight back and it will feel like you are dragging your lead over smooth concrete. No kicks, plucks or tremors will be felt and the longer this lasts, the larger the clear spot is.

Whilst it's very easy to be impressed with all the fancy end tackles and presentations that are around today, it is impossible to decide on which is the correct rig to use until you know the depth of the water you are fishing in and the nature of the lake bed you are casting onto. To do this can take up to an hour but it is time well spent. Your rig may spend many hours out in the swim and if it's the incorrect one, purely and simply because you didn't take the time to feature find, you are not making the most of your time or understanding the importance of feature finding. Don't let it happen - work at your fishing. However, always remember that excessive disturbance of your swim can temporarily scare the fish out of the area, so avoid doing it if the session is to be a very short one - better to make a special trip to the water before hand, or do another area of the lake which you intend to fish next time.

For additional information on feature finding and general "water craft" consult the books, *Carp Fever* and the *Beekay Guide to Starting Carp Fishing*.

3. Components

Not so long ago it would have almost been possible to list all the different kinds of hooks, leads, hooklinks and so on available and how to use each to best effect. However, with the boom in carp fishing the availability of products has increased incredibly and it is not feasible or sensible to carry out such a list. Instead we shall detail all the components used in the end tackles, presentations and suchlike in this book and restrict our recommendations to items we use. Of course, there are many good alternatives available and we are not for one moment telling you that you have to use each of our stated choices instead of your own. If you have a particular favourite and it is not letting you down, don't change it. Be aware of the alternatives available and change only if you think it would be an advantage to do so.

HOOKLENGTH MATERIAL

There is an excellent selection of hooklength materials available for today's carp angler, and whatever form of presentation you choose to use you are more than well catered for. Most of the featured presentations include a hooklength from one of the following materials.

a) Monofilament - for standard monofilament hooklengths you can use a normal monofilament such as Sylcast, Maxima or Brent or if you require a specialist monofilament hooklength which has a high abrasion resistance you can use Berkley Trilene XT (extra tough) or for suppleness Berkley Trilene XL (extra limp). Another useful nylon is Carp 'R' Us Ghost, which is virtually invisible in water and is slightly heavier than standard monofilaments. Whatever monofilament you do decide to choose equip yourself with breaking strains between 6 and 17 pounds.

b) Stiff Monofilament - for making up stiff rigs you can use standard monofilament in 15 to 30 pounds or you can use a product called Amnesia shooting head line in 20 to 30 pounds or Ghost available in 20 pounds.

c) Braids - for many carp fishing presentations a supple braid will suffice and many companies sell them. Most braids are very good indeed and we can highly recommend Kryston's Merlin and Silkworm braid in 8, 10, 12, 15 and 25 pound rating, Richworth's Sorceror, and the equiva-

Dacron and nylon looping all over the place! Can you spot Silkworm's
amazing camouflage in the bottom left of the picture held down with
a tiny spot of Magma?

lents from Kesmark and Carp 'R' Us. Most braids come on 20 metre and
40 metre spools and as you will use quite a large amount of braid each
season it's best to purchase the larger, more economical spools. They
also eventually deteriorate when immersed in water time and time again
so be careful when using the same hooklength week in week out, or it
may let you down. Better to chop it off and tie on a new one.

d) Multistrands - for combi-links Kryston's twisted Multistrand is an
excellent aid to presentation and being almost undetectable in water
offers your hookbait a high degree of free movement which supple
braids cannot match. For those people who are unhappy tying a combi-
link knot, Kesmark's Combi-Splice is excellent, plus Relum, Kryston,
and Carp 'R' Us have products on sale which allow you to push back and
snip off the outer core of braid revealing a section of multistrand. This
is equally as good as the standard combi-link which requires you to knot
the braid and the multistrand together.

MAINLINE

No one mainline will cover all eventualities and what may well suffice for
fishing in weed can be unsuitable for casting long distances with. For that
reason it's best to spool up, or at least have in your possession various
types of mainline.

The Withy Pool version of the sliding ring rig with pop-up
accounted for this $33\frac{1}{2}$ pound mirror.

a) For standard carp fishing - Sylcast Sorrel in 11 and 15 pounds rating or
   Berkley Big Game in 12 or 15 pounds rating.
b) For distance fishing - Brent Sorrel in 8 or 10 pounds rating, Maxima in
   10 pounds rating, Sylcast in 9 or 11 pounds or Berkley Trilene XL in 8
   or 12 pounds rating.
c) For fishing in weed or to snags - Berkley Trilene XT in 14 or 17 pounds
   rating, Sylcast Sorrel in 15 pounds rating or Berkley Big Game in 15
   pounds rating (Specimen Brown version).

SHOCKLEADERS

When you fish at range you will need to use a shockleader to absorb the
force of the cast. Various shockleaders are available but the following are
our favourites.

Kryston Quicksilver in 25, 35 or 45 pounds rating, Berkley Trilene
XT in 17 pounds or Sylcast Sorrel in 18 pounds rating.

LEAD CORE LEADER

To fish the lead core presentation you need a reliable lead core to mount
your end tackle on. We recommend:

One of a brace of mid-winter 30's which fell to single hookbaits
soaked in Strawberry SR35 oil.

Carp 'R' Us Ledkor in 25 and 35 pounds, or Cortland Kerplunk lead
core fly line in 27 or 36 pounds rating.

HOOKS

There are literally hundreds to choose from and each year sees new addi-
tions to the range. However, for the purposes of the presentations detailed
in this book you should obtain some or all of the following:-

Drennan Super Specimen Hook	(Size 4-10)
Partridge Z15 Kevin Maddocks Boilie Hook	(Size 4-8)
Ashima C-310 Carp Hook	(Size 4-8)
Mustad O'Shaunessey 34021 Hook	(Size 4-8)
Frank Warwick Cranked Hook	(Size 4-8)
Fox series 1, 2 and 3	(Size 2-8)
Partridge Z11 Kevin Maddocks Hair Rig Hook	(Size 4-8)
Carp 'R' Us Centurion 2000	(Size 4-8)
Carp 'R' Us Amnesia D rig hook	(Size 4-8)
Carp 'R' Us Lightweight Swimmer rig hook	(Size 4-8)

Whatever hook you do decide to use always check it thoroughly before you tie it to your hooklength. Whilst most hooks are excellent, bad ones do occur and they can cost you fish. Check that the eyes are closed properly, the barb properly formed and the point is not blunted. Never be tempted to use a hook many times and after catching a fish or between sessions it is often best to change your hook. Hooks can rust which will cause them to snap and points can turn over after repeated use.

HOOK SHARPENERS

Most hooks available today come needle-sharp out of the packet but there are occasions when you need to sharpen a hook slightly. Walkers of Trowell do an excellent hook sharpener which can be used on hooks down to size 12.

When you take your hook from the packet, check it is needle-sharp and, if necessary, use your hook sharpener gently to perfect it. However, if the hook is blunt or malformed, don't try to sharpen it; throw it away and use another one. If you don't, you may end up creating a short chisel point which will not have the same ability to penetrate. The same applies to hooks during actual fishing sessions. If it appears not to be needle-sharp discard the presentation and use a new one as many of the latest chemically sharpened hooks are useless once sharpened. Don't ruin what would otherwise be an excellent carp presentation for the sake of a hook.

SWIVELS

Very few swivels act perfectly but this really has little influence on how your rig will perform once cast out. Providing the swivel does allow the hooklength to rotate or swivel and does not crush the knot and is strong enough to land the carp, it will suffice. Most presentations included in this book use:-

Berkley size 5, 7 or 10 swivels
American Bear swivels in 40 or 60 pound test

HAIRLENGTHS

Many of the presentations included utilise a hair rig of one type or another. These are the hair materials used in those presentations:-

Unwaxed dental floss which is available from most major chemists or if in difficulty use hair braid under Kesmark or Fox ranges. Flosses have an advantage over nylon in that when immersed in water the strands separate and allow the hookbait a high degree of free movement. It becomes almost invisible in water which can be an advantage when fishing for wary carp. You can also use Kryston's Multistrand as a hairlength as it offers your hookbait a great deal of free movement.

Bayer Perlon 1.1 or 1.7 pound monofilament. For standard hair rigs this fine monofilament is ideal.

ANTI-TANGLE TUBING

When using standard monofilament you do not need to use anti-tangle tubing as the hooklength should not wrap round the mainline in mid flight; this can sometimes be a distict advantage if you wish to reduce the amount of 'garbage' around your end tackle! However, when using soft monofilaments, braids and combi-links, it is essential to use anti-tangle tubing to avoid the hooklength wrapping round the mainline in flight. Various types of anti-tangle tubing are available but the end tackles in this book use:-

Terry Eustace Gold Label $\frac{1}{2}$ mm rig tube in black or muddy green
Armatube Anti-Tangle tubing in 1 mm
Mainlinks Camouflaged Rig Tubing in $\frac{1}{2}$ mm to 2 mm
Carp 'R' Us Barrier Tubing in 1mm

As well as anti-tangle tubing you will need various other pieces of silicon tubing to act as lead sleeves etc. The rigs detailed later use:-

Mainlink Link Sleeves $1\frac{1}{2}$ mm and 2 mm
Terry Eustace Gold Label rig tube 2 mm and 3 mm
Streamselect Tadpole Rubbers

LEADS

There are many excellent leads available but for all the end tackles detailed we use:-

Korda Distance Casting Leads - $2\frac{1}{2}$ and 3 ounce	(70-85g)
Korda Pear Lead - $1\frac{1}{2}$, $2\frac{1}{2}$ and $3\frac{1}{2}$ ounce	(42-100g)
Korda In-Line Leads - 3 and $3\frac{1}{2}$ ounce	(85-100g)
Streamselect Attracta Lead - 2, 3 and 4 ounce	(55-115g)
Streamselect Through Attracta Lead - 3 and $3\frac{1}{2}$ ounce	(85-100g)
M.C.F. Developments In-Line lead - 2, $2\frac{1}{2}$, 3 and $3\frac{1}{2}$ ounce	(55-100g)
Carp 'R' Us Profile Lead - 2, $2\frac{1}{2}$, 3 and $3\frac{1}{2}$ ounce	(55-100g)

SHRINK TUBE

Many of the rigs which incorporate line aligners and the like require you to use shrink tube. All the later detailed presentations utilise:-

Terry Eustace Gold Label Shrink Tube - Nos 1, 2 and 3
    (in clear or black)

A standard bottom bait proved more effective than a pop-up set up
for this margin caught mid-30.

Kesmark Shrink Tube (in clear and black)
Carp 'R' Us Shrink Tube 2.5mm (Shrinks down to .8mm)

These will allow you to form line aligners on all hooks between size 2 and
size 12.

BOILY STOPS

When piercing your bait and threading it on a hair you will need to use a
hairstop to keep it on. Several manufacturers make excellent versions in
colours to match your bait.

BALANCING AIDS

For pop-up rigs and the like you will need various balancing aids to hold
your bait, hooklength, and so on down.

Kryston Heavy Metal or Carp 'R' Us Ballast - lead putty to balance
baits and hold down some types of tubing.

Kryston Snag Safe - putty which pulls off when fishing in
    snaggy/weedy areas.
Kryston Magma - liquid lead weight to hold down hooklengths.
Carp 'R' Us Featherweight slow sink putty.
Shot - in size 8 to AAA to mould the putty round.

GLUES

Various glues and resins designed for the carp market are available and
although it is possible to use standard superglue, it is best to also have the
following specific products:-

Kryston Hawser - to stiffen braids as and when necessary.
Kryston Superstiff Gel - to allow you to cast out multistrand hook-
    lengths without fear of a tangle.
Kesmark Octo-Gel - for blobbing hooks and gluing parts of your
    rig.
Kevin Nash Rig Glue - for gluing parts of your rig this is excellent
    as it dispenses the glue in single drops.
Carp 'R' Us Rig Glue Pen.
Kryston Greased Lightning Turbo Juice - this allows friction free
    casting and increases your casting range.
Kryston Granite Juice - for protecting your mainline.

PRESENTATION AIDS

To cover all eventualities you will need to have the following available in
your tackle box:-

Cork balls - for use as alternative mixers when floater fishing.
Poly balls - for use in making pop-up or balanced boilies.
Kryston Bogey - to enable you to present a ball of seeds as a hook-
    bait.
Line grease - to enable you to keep your hooklength on the surface
    when fishing floating baits.
Kryston Driftwood or Carp 'R' Us Iceburg - a floating putty which
    will pull free from your mainline if it comes into contact with
    weed/snags.
Wine corks - for simple controller rigs.

Also don't forget to take a container to balance your baits in, as paddling
about in the margins is not advisable! Purchase a clear container which is
at least 10 inches deep, and once it is filled with water you can do a proper
balancing or overshotting job without having to rush it.

POWERGUM

Gardner powergum in 7, 11 and 22 pounds rating or Fox camouflaged powergum

DRILLS AND NEEDLES

Gardner Stringer Needle - providing your boilies are not too hard, this is ideal.

Solar Boilie & Stop Needle - ideal for very hard boilies as length of needle can be adjusted.

Drennan Nut Drill - to drill holes in mixers or particles this is excellent.

Kesmark Splicing Needle and Threaders - for splicing Octo-Splice and lead core leaders.

CUTTING AIDS

A good pair of scissors will suffice but due to the tough nature of some braids you would be best advised to possess the following:-

Clippers - for close monofilament trimming.

Fox Braid Scissors - to trim braids and leaders neatly.

PVA

Later in the book we will cover extensively the use of PVA in carp rigs but in order to follow those ideas you need to obtain certain items.

Kryston Meltdown PVA string.

Kesmark Vanish PVA String, fine or dense.

Kevin Nash Top Rod PVA stringer tape

Kevin Nash Top Rod rig bags

Kevin Nash Top Rod hook bait bags

Streamselect dissolving flavour tablets

Carp 'R' Us Cobweb PVA bags and tape

BEADS

A selection from Mainline's range of rubber shocker beads and standard helicopter beads is vital to cover all eventualities. Both Gold Label Tackle and Ivel Products also supply some excellent beads for use in plumbing set-ups etc. Also some large bore run rings are essential for running lead end tackles.

FLOATS

A selection of Drennan crystal wagglers and bodied wagglers. Small trotting floats for close range stalking. For floater fishing Kevin Nash controllers in 70, 100 and 130 gramme weights. For plumbing Drennan, Ivel or Fox marker floats.

TACKLE BOXES AND RIG WALLETS

To keep all these products in and to make sure you are ready to fish as soon as you reach the water, it is vital that you have a good tackle box and rig wallet.

1. Rig wallets. These allow you to tie your presentations up in advance and store them for use in the future. You can also leave your bait on the tied-up presentation if you keep the rig wallet in the freezer. A number of companies do sell them.
2. Rig boards. If you are using stiff rigs you don't want to have your stiff link bent in circles so you would be best advised to keep tied-up versions on a rig board. You can also use this board with its pins for standard braid presentations. Use either Kevin Nash's or Fox Tackle's versions.
3. Tackle boxes. To store all your items, such as braids, hooks, putty and the like, you need to obtain a good sized tackle box. Whatever version you decide to obtain do ensure it will fit into your current choice of rucksack. You will be amazed at how many items you will need so you will need to take a decent sized one. Again, a number of good tackle boxes are available on the market such as the Fox System Select. Later in the book we've detailed how to use many of these components to tie up a number of presentations. However, if you are inexperienced you can buy excellent ready tied rigs from Kesmark or Carp 'R' Us range. These cover all types of presentations from stiff rigs to combi-links and save you having to purchase lots of separate components.

Of course there are probably many other items which you could utilise in carp rigs today but rest assured if you possess the ones we've detailed you will be able to tie up all the later detailed end tackles and presentations.

4. Knots and Suchlike

No matter which rig you decide to use it will inevitably have at least one knot in its make-up and often many more. You may well have the ideal hook, the correct sized lead and perfect hooklength but if your knot fails all that goes to waste. The following knots are proven for the end tackles and presentations we've detailed – learn how to tie them, practise and never have to worry again about unnecessary fish losses.

1. Braid Knot (Fig. 6)

BRAID TO SWIVEL – BRAID TO HOOK

This is known as a five turn grinner knot. Although you can actually use only four turns a five turn one gives that extra bit of security. Ensure that the whole knot is wetted as you draw it together and if the coils overlap each other and bunch up cut it off and start again. Note that the braid has gone twice through the eye before you make your loops – this makes an appreciable difference.

Fig. 6. Braid Knot

2. Monofilament Knots (Fig. 7)

MONOFILAMENT TO SWIVEL – MONOFILAMENT TO HOOK

There are a variety of knots that you can use to knot monofilament line up to 20 pounds. One we would advise you to use is what's known as a five turn clinch knot which seems to be a little more reliable than the standard five turn blood knot which is very popular. Another excellent knot is the KM Blood Knot (first featured in Carp Fever) which is passed twice through the eye, then five turns around the mainline and the end is fed back through the gap above the eye of the hook (see diagram). Always wet your monofilament thoroughly before tightening down and if the line is crinkly or crushed you must discard it and try again until it's right.

When using very heavy line to form a stiff rig you do not need to use a clinch knot and a standard three turn blood knot or three turn KM Blood knot will suffice. Because of the thickness of the stiff monofilament it would be almost impossible to do a five turn blood knot. Once you've tied the knot slide it down until there is a loop formed approximately one inch

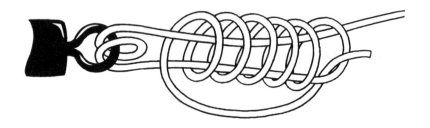

Fig. 7(a). The Monofilament Knot

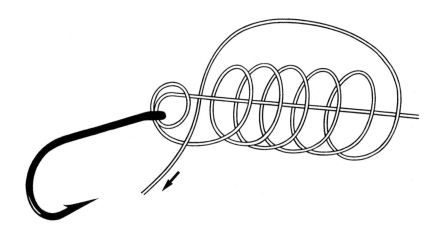

Fig. 7(b). The KM Blood Knot

in diameter. This creates the loop or hinge which makes the stiff rig so effective (Fig.8). If you still feel a little unconfident about using just a three turn knot, you could always add a small blob of superglue to secure it. Also slide a little piece of fine diameter rig tubing down the stiff link to cover that knot. It neatens it up considerably and cuts down on the likelyhood of a tangle on the snipped monofilament.

3. Shockleader Knot (Fig. 9)

MAINLINE TO SHOCKLEADER PROVIDING IT IS NOT LEAD CORE FLY LINE

This is a very simple knot but one which is very easy to tie incorrectly. For that reason alone many carp anglers give up on shockleaders. As with all knots wet thoroughly and slide gently. If you are using monofilament to monofilament it's no problem providing you take care to avoid bunching and slipping. However, if you are knotting monofilament to a Kryston Quicksilver leader you must take great care to completely wet the monofilament so it slides snuggly against the Quicksilver knot. Don't pull the coils of monofilament tight until they are almost against the thick leader knot; because Quicksilver is quite rough, monofilament doesn't slide so easy over it. You can improve the security of the shockleader knot by coating it

Whatever rig you choose must be able to land the carp in your swim.

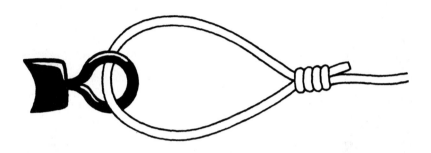

Fig. 8. Loop effect

Fig. 9. Shockleader Knot

in a light covering of Kryston's Hawser but this can cut down casting distance due to the increased size of the knot. Do not use superglue or it will stiffen the trimmed ends up rock solid and these will jam in the tip ring causing crack offs.

4. Combi-link Knot (Fig.10)

MULTISTRAND TO BRAID

If you decide to use the combi-link for fishing and don't want to use purpose made combi-link braids, you need to master this knot. It's a simple four turn water knot and is very easy to tie. As with all knots wet thoroughly before you draw the knot together and if it does not hold 100% correctly re-do it until it is right. For added security coat the knot in Kryston's Hawser and leave it overnight to dry.

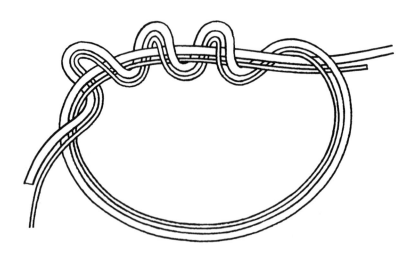

Fig. 10. Combi-link Knot (Four turn Water Knot)

5. Multistrand Knot (Fig.11)

MULTISTRAND TO HOOK – MULTISTRAND TO SWIVEL

When using multistrand as a hooklength in its own right you need to use a special version of the grinner knot. Instead of the normal four to six turns

Fig. 11. Two turn Grinner (Multistrand Knot)

you only use two; this stops strangulation which can be a problem with multistrands. Put the multistrand only once through the eye and follow it up with only two turns for the grinner part of it. You will find it easier to tie multistrand knots if you gently wet the material first; this helps to ensure all the strands are taken up evenly, which is essential for a good knot. Once you've tied this knot test it thoroughly to make sure it doesn't slip under pressure. If you do not feel happy using this knot, another proven one for multistrands and flosses is the clinch knot we detailed earlier when looking at how to knot monofilament.

6. Lead Core Fly Line Knot (Fig.12)

LEAD CORE TO MONOFILAMENT

Although there are a number of different knots you can use to do this, many have the inherent problem that the knot they create is bulky and will not allow your tubing or beads to pass over it if you crack off; such a rig would be a death rig. The best knot to use is a needle knot and although it looks a little complicated it is very effective indeed, very neat and 100% reliable when tied correctly. It's not a technique you can master easily when you first start to tie it, so practise it at home until you can tie it proficiently. Whilst the needle knot will attach your lead core fly line leader

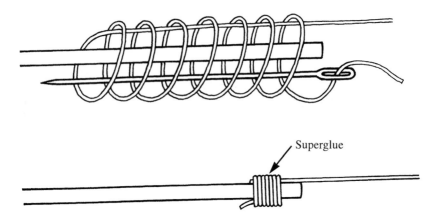

Fig. 12. Needle Knot for attaching mono to lead core fly line

to the monofilament mainline, to attach the lead core to your swivel all you need to do is tie a very basic three turn blood knot. Take the lead core out of the braid surround, use the three turn blood knot to attach it to the swivel and add a drop of Kryston's Hawser or superglue to hold it securely.

7. Hair Rig Knot (Fig.13)

TO FORM A LOOP FOR YOUR BOILY STOP

Whilst you can use a very simple overhand knot to form the hair, a better way is to use a crochet needle to pull the knot through on itself. This will not slip and does not need superglue or a second knot to hold it securely.

If your pop-up is rock hard and you cannot get a boily needle through it, you will need to use a dental floss loop knot to hold it on (Fig.14). Providing you use unwaxed dental floss and tie the knot correctly, it cannot slacken – it can only tighten up and become even more secure. With this knot you can cast as hard as you want and the bait won't come off. Remember that once in the water the bait will swell slightly so drawing the knot into it making it absolutely secure.

To attach the hair to the eye of the hook use a simple double granny knot. There is no need to use any fancy knots as the tube will hold it securely. If you feel unhappy about that add a drop of superglue.

Fig. 13. Hair Rig Knot

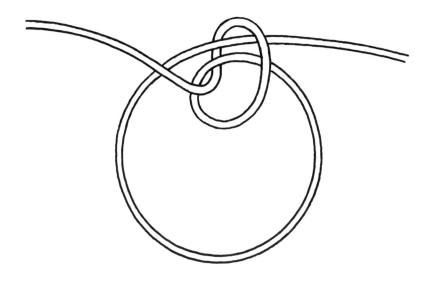

Fig. 14. Dental Floss Loop for Pop-up

Fig. 15. Sliding Slip Knot

8. Sliding Stop Knot (Fig.15)

FOR MARKER FLOAT USE OR TO MOULD LEAD PUTTY ROUND

This is also known as a slip knot and is very useful. You can use either braid or powergum to tie the knot and both are equally good. No matter which you choose to use always wet the line it is being put on before you pull it tight. Also, if you want to move the stop knot up or down, wet the mainline so it does not crease that mainline or burn through your knot. If you want to use thick powergum for your stop knot you do not have to use five or six turns for your stop knot, three will do.

9. Knotless Hook Knot (Fig.16)

MONOFILAMENT OR BRAID TO HOOK

To avoid using a knot in the conventional sense you can use what is known as a knotless hook knot. It creates a very strong hold indeed and a hair as well. Also because of the nature of the knot it causes a flip over effect like the line aligner which aids in hooking carp.

TESTING KNOTS

No matter which knot you do decide to use you must always test it properly before you cast out. It may look good, it may feel good but nothing

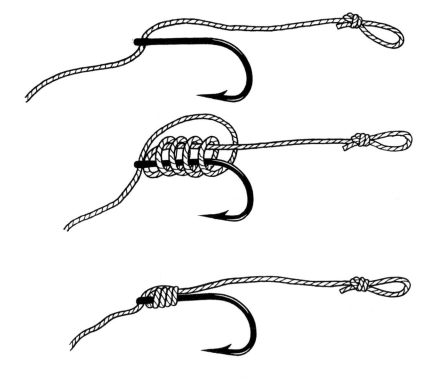

Fig. 16. The "Knotless" Hook Knot

Gravel pit fish can demand fine tuning of presentation.

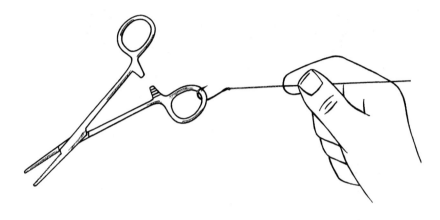

Fig. 17. Incorrect knot testing

can match a correct knot test. Do not just stick it in your forceps and yank; that's a sure-fire way of opening out your hook by placing all the strain on the bend of the hook and not on the knot itself (Fig.17). As the diagrams illustrate grip the hook securely with your forceps and gently bed that knot down and then test it with some force (Fig.18).

THE LINE ALIGNER

Whilst the line aligner is not a knot as such, because it is so effective and so popular it is important that we detail how to tie it up properly so that you can utilise its full potential.

When your hook, hair and hookbait are taken into the carp's mouth it is essential that the hook finds a hold somewhere in the mouth of the carp. By using a line aligner, the hook is much more likely to snag inside the carp's mouth once inside than a standard knot on the eye. This is because the hooklength comes out at an angle and causes the hook to flip over and take hold in the bottom lip. Much like the bent hook, this line aligner "flip over" effect is very useful when the carp are somewhat wary of standard presentations and you need to go one step further to hook them.

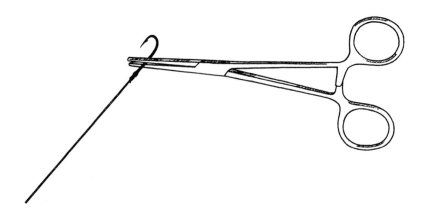

Fig. 18. Correct knot testing

For most of the presentations we detail, a conventional line aligner will suffice and here's how we tie one up.

1. First of all, tie your hook as normal and trim the remaining braid off (Fig.19).
2. Mount your bottom bait or pop-up on a dental floss hair or loop and tie it to the eye of the hook so it hangs as you want it to (Fig.20).
3. Cut off a piece of shrink tube, slide a fine needle down it and exit the tube through its wall about $\frac{1}{4}$" (6mm) from the end (Fig.21).
4. Thread your braid through the eye of the needle and pull the needle through the tube so your hooklength follows it. Unthread the needle.
5. Slide the shrink tube down the hooklength and over the eye so it covers the hookshank as illustrated (Fig.22).
6. Add steam to the shrink tube until a firm line aligner is formed (Fig.23). You don't always have to use shrink tube as standard rig tube can also be used for line- aligners.

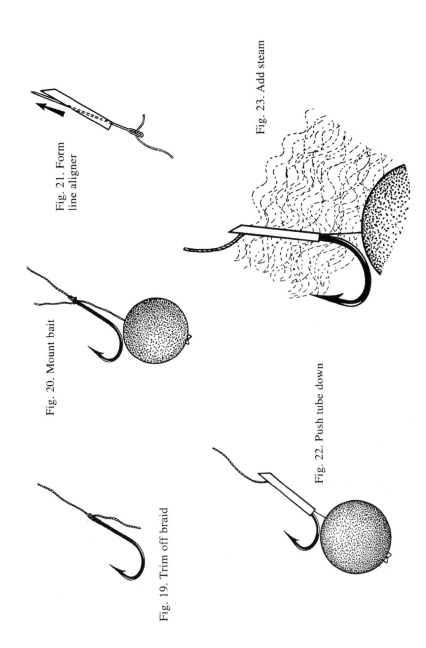

Fig. 23. Add steam

Fig. 21. Form line aligner

Fig. 20. Mount bait

Fig. 22. Push tube down

Fig. 19. Trim off braid

Nice 20 using a PVA bag.

5. Indication Matters!

No matter which carp rig you do decide to use, it's very important that you fish that rig on the correct indication system. For even if your rig does allow the carp to pick up the bait and hook itself, if your indication system is poor, or poorly set up, you may miss the take and the carp may escape without you even knowing you've had a pick-up. From mainline to buzzer, from backlead to visual indicator – indication matters!

ITEMS THAT INFLUENCE INDICATION

a) Mainline – this has a far greater effect than many people imagine. All mainlines have a degree of stretch in them and as you cast further out there is more line out in the water and consequently more "stretch" out there. This "stretch" will absorb indications of a take and the further out you are the worse it is. For that reason if possible when fishing at range try not to use a line with too much stretch in it or you may find small indications go unnoticed. Obviously you need to balance that with the need to choose the correct line in all the circumstances. Also whilst a strong line does give you greater control over the carp when playing it you cannot tighten up quite as well on such a line which will affect indication. The finer the line the more indication you will get of a take on your buzzer or visual indicator.

b) Buzzer – it should go without saying that the more sensitive your audible indicator is the better. The top of the range buzzers like Delkims and Fox DXR's pick up any vibration on your line and do not require line to be taken and moved. Whilst some self hooked carp do scream off giving a fast run, on many occasions you may only get a vibration. Also if you are fishing at long range the line stretch may absorb a short take and you may only end up with vibration at the angler's end. Having a top grade buzzer can produce bonus fish in such circumstances. If you don't have one of these types of buzzers always try to make your correct choice of buzzer as sensitive as you can. Some manufacturers sell spare wheels/blades which effectively increase the sensitivity of the buzzer; these are well worth investing in. Ensure your indicator is in good working order at all times.

c) Banksticks – it's essential that your buzzers and buzzer bars are stable at all times so that you don't get any false indications in the wind from bankstick sway. The lower your rods and reels are to the ground the less chance of bankstick sway there is, so look for banksticks around 16 inches (40cm) or so. Many firms make excellent banksticks with Fox, Obelisk and Solar Tackle being particularly good.

d) Buzzer Bars – to mount your buzzers on you need good quality buzzer bars. When fishing two rods a buzzer bar which has one bankstick in the middle of it is fine. However, when you use a three rod set-up it is better to use the buzzer bars which allow you to screw a bankstick into each end of them. This creates a solid set-up and when using powerful rods and large reels it's vital or your set-up will sway. The bars are known as dual bars and are made by Obelisk and one or two other companies. Alternatively, you can use a single bankstick in conjunction with a stabiliser which pushed into the ground and can be tightened to the bankstick – Solar Tackle produce an excellent adjustable stabiliser.

e) Rear Butt Grips – as well as ensuring your rods rest firmly on your buzzers, it's important to make sure the butt of your rod is held firmly, so that it cannot slide or twist. Many companies make excellent rear rod grips such as the Fox Rod-Locs and John Roberts rubber butt grip. Particularly good are Solar and Obelisk versions which incorporate velcro on the butt grip and rod handle. This holds the rod securely during takes but allows you to lift it clear and strike.

f) Rod Pods – whilst occasionally you may have to fish waters which have hard banks so requiring the use of rod pods, the said items should not be used as a matter of practice. Certainly rod pods have their uses but many do not allow you to angle your rods for maximum indicator sensitivity. This can restrict those subtle takes and could cost you carp. Use a rod pod when you have to but don't become a slave to them. Fox, Solar and Obelisk versions are recommended.

g) Monkey Climbers – these used to be a very popular type of visual indicator but do have their limitations in today's carp scene. The main problem with monkey climbers is that whilst a take from a carp will pull the line in one direction (or two if it's a drop back) the movement of the bobbin can only be at right angles to that. As you can see from the drawing (Fig.24) this creates a great deal of friction which is not ideal and can mean you miss the more subtle takes. For long range fishing where you may encounter drop backs, very heavy bobbins on a monkey climber do have their uses.

h) Hanging Bobbins – these were one of the original visual indicators used by carp anglers and having been "rediscovered" in the last few years have proved to be very useful indeed. All you do is clip them to your mainline (Fig.25) and any movements at all should register quite dramatically on them. Because there is no swinging arm or monkey (which is to their advantage as it allows almost 100% unhindered free movement) they are very susceptible to wind and drag. For that reason they are best used for fishing at under 40 yards; to fish further out you'd need

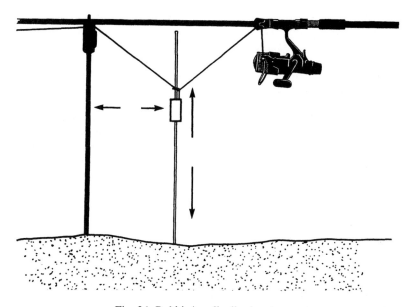

Fig. 24. Bobbin/needle disadvantages

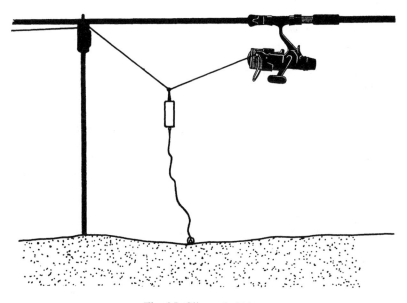

Fig. 25. Clip-on bobbin

a heavier bobbin. Many companies make excellent hanging bobbins.

i) Swinging Arm Indicators – Richard Walker invented the first of these about 20 years ago but then bite indication was not so important and the "Nightjar", as it was called, was not popular and was soon withdrawn from the market. However, these are very popular today and not without good cause as they offer an acceptable and usable compromise between the monkey climber and the hanging bobbin. The swinging arm offers far more sensitivity than a monkey climber but unlike the hanging bobbin it is not affected by wind and drift. Most swinging arm indicators have a range of sensitivities available which can be adjusted by moving the counterweight, cam etc (Fig.26). For standard carp fishing situations where you are fishing at distances up to 70 yards a Fox Mark I swinger is ideal whilst for longer range fishing a Fox Springer or Solar Quiver-Loc would be a better choice. Although swinging arm indicators are very popular nowadays do not be a slave to them and use them when suitable and other visual indicators for different situations.

j) Backleads – later in this chapter we will look specifically at how to use backleads to your advantage but in order to be able to tackle all situations it would be advisable to be in possession of a range of backleads. Several companies have an excellent range of backleads to cover all situations, including Carp 'R' Us Flyback Tungsten Tube.

k) Line Clips – for tight lining which we will cover later, you need to have with you a selection of quality line clips. Some rods have line clips built onto them already but if your rod does not, then Solar Tackle sell excellent line clips to cover all types of rods.

HOW TO SET UP YOUR INDICATION SYSTEM CORRECTLY

Having purchased and fine tuned all the necessary components for effective indication, it's now important to consider the various ways you can arrange your rod, reel, buzzers and visual indicators for maximum indication. Of course, you can just cast out, clip on your indicator and switch on your buzzer and hope, but if you take the time to set them up you may catch more fish. No one set-up will cater for all occasions so let's look at the various ones available.

1. The use of single banksticks – in order to maximise indication your rod needs to be pointed directly at your baited end tackle. This straight line greatly improves movement of your line so increasing audible and visual indication (Fig.27). Obviously, there will be occasions when you cannot point your rod at the end tackle (baits down the margins, restricted swim etc) but if you can it's always best to fish your rods on single banksticks and pointing directly at the hookbait. Clearly, when fishing at long range straight out in front of you a standard buzzer bar set-up will suffice as any angle is negligible.

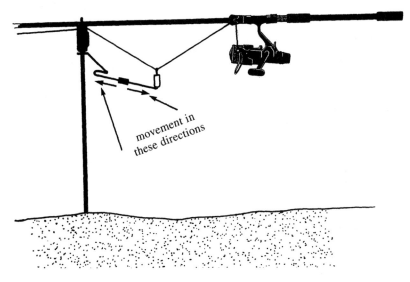

Fig. 26. Swinging arm indicator

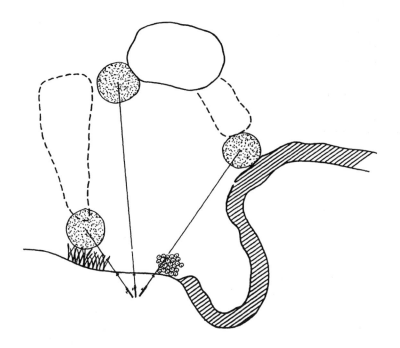

Fig. 27. Use of single bank sticks

CARP VIDEOS

WITHY POOL: Carp Water Supreme - Kevin Maddocks	£13.99
PRACTICAL CARPING 1: Julian Cundiff	£13.99
PRACTICAL CARPING 2: Julian Cundiff	£13.99
PRACTICAL CARPING 3: Julian Cundiff	£13.99
PRACTICAL CARPING 4: Julian Cundiff	£13.99
BIG CARP CHALLENGE 1: Mid Northants - Alan Taylor	£13.99
BIG CARP CHALLENGE 2: Horton - Alan Taylor	£13.99
FRENCH CARPING: An Introduction - Alan Taylor	£13.99
FRENCH CARPING 1: River Seine - Marc Ponsot & Friends	£13.99
FRENCH CARPING 2: Ton-Up, Lac Du Der - A.Taylor & Friends	£13.99
FRENCH CARPING 3: Chantecoq Facts - A.Taylor & K. Maddocks	£13.99
FRENCH CARPING 4: Big Carp, Orient - Kevin Maddocks	£13.99
FRENCH CARPING 5: Successful Failure - P.Regent & K.Bishop	£13.99
CARP FEVER 1: The Carp Revolution - Kevin Maddocks	£12.99
CARP FEVER 2: Rigs & Baits - Kevin Maddocks	£12.99
CARP FEVER 3: Baits & Rigs - Kevin Maddocks	£12.99
CARP FEVER 4: Off The Top & Down Below - Kevin Maddocks	£14.99
COLD-WATER CARPING: Kevin Maddocks	£13.99
ITALY: Basic Carping - Kevin Maddocks	£13.99
ITALY: Advanced Carping - Kevin Maddocks	£13.99
LONG RANGE CARPING: Phil Hyde & Clive Gibbins	£13.99
CARP TEACH - IN: Andy Little & Friends	£13.99
CARP FISHING: (Cuttle Mill) - Des Taylor	£13.99
STALKING CARP: (On Floaters) - Des Taylor	£13.99
EURO CARP QUEST 1: Fishabil - Kevin Maddocks	£12.99
EURO CARP QUEST 2: Brive - Kevin Maddocks	£12.99

BEST SELLERS

EXPEDITION BELUGA: (Sturgeon To 273lbs) - Kevin Maddocks	£13.99
CATFISH TOUR OF EUROPE: (Double Pack 2 x 60mins) - Kevin Maddocks	£19.99
BIG CATS OF THE VOLGA: Kevin Maddocks	£12.99
TENCH FISHING: David Maddocks	£13.99

*All these videos can be purchased or ordered via your local tackle shop
if you find this not possible, you can obtain them direct from Beekay -
simply add £1 per item for P+P.*

BEEKAY INTERNATIONAL

**Withy Pool, Henlow Camp,
Beds, SG16 6EA.
Tel: 01462 816960
Fax: 01462 817253**

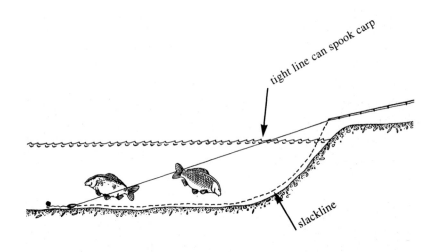

Fig. 28. Slack lining

2. Slack lining – on some waters carp are very wary of main lines in mid
   water which brush against them (Fig.28) and this can cause them to
   spook or feed cautiously in the baited area. This is particularly true of
   pressurised carp or carp in clear open waters which are not used to anything brushing against their flanks. In weed the carp may well be used
   to movement against their body but in non-weedy gravel pits it's a completely different story. To avoid the carp coming into contact with your
   mainline a tactic called slack lining is used. To do it is very easy indeed.
   First of all cast out and make sure that the baited end tackle is in exactly the right spot. As soon as it hits the bottom at the right spot, flick your
   bale arm over and take in the slack carefully. Your rod rests and buzzers
   need to be set as low as possible and your rod tip needs to be back from
   the water's edge to avoid margin patrolling carp coming into contact
   with them. Put your rod in its rests and let the line settle. Now clip on
   your visual indicator. This will tension the line somewhat. Undo your
   clutch or click on your baitrunner facility and start to pay out line until
   the line at the rod tip hangs limply. All the line from under the rod tip to
   the end tackle will now be laid along the lake bed in a tactic called slack
   lining. This is an excellent method when the carp are wary of lines in
   mid water but it needs to be considered carefully before you use it.
   Because there is so much slack line out, the carp may pick the bait up
   and bolt before the angler is aware of it. This can lead to snagged or
   weeded fish. Because there is no tension to pull the hook home you are

A good winter fish on scaled down tackle.

relying solely on the weight of the lead. Hooks need to be razor sharp and leads at least three ounces (85g) in weight. Always remember that with this method you will get no indication of a fish running towards you if using a fixed lead, so for close range slack lining a fixed lead is acceptable but for medium to long range a heavy sliding lead will give better bite indication.

3. Standard set-up – on many waters at ranges up to 70 yards this is the ideal way to set up your rods and it's an ideal compromise between slack lining and tight lining. Cast out and wait until the lead hits exactly the right spot. Once it has done, flick over your bale arm and take in the slack line carefully by reeling in gently. Once that slack has been taken in put your rod in its rests. If possible the rod should be on two single rests and pointing directly at the end tackle. Now undo the clutch a little and by hand keep tensioning the line and winding the slack in via the clutch. Once the line is quite tight, clip on your visual indicator (Fig.29). The tension in your line will mean that the indicator is tight against the rod. Undo your clutch a little, or click on your baitrunner, and start to pay out line carefully. As line goes out the tension will ease a little and the visual indicator will start to drop. When it is level with your reel spool this is ideal. Any movement at all, be it a take or a drop back, will register quite dramatically on this finely balanced set-up. This is ideal for most situations and due to its sensitivity it's nicknamed the "slightest touch" method.

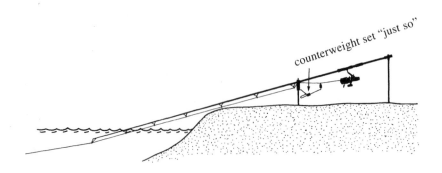

counterweight set "just so"

Fig. 29. Standard set-up

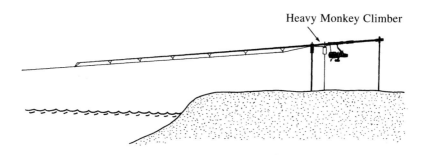

Heavy Monkey Climber

Fig. 30. Tight lining

4. Tight lining – in direct comparison with slack lining is the method known as tight lining. This is where you use as tight a line as possible to pull the hook home. On easy waters, at long range, or even on waters which haven't seen its use for some time, it can catch carp out. Use the heaviest lead you have which you can safely and accurately cast out. Once it's in exactly the right spot, take in the slack by winding in with your reel. Now put your rod in its rest. Your rod should be low to the ground and pointing exactly at the end tackle to ensure maximum registration. Undo your clutch a little and start to claw in line inch by inch. Keep doing this until your mainline is as tight as you can possibly make it. You should be able to feel the lead and the line should be bowstring tight. Now clip on your visual indicator which ideally would be a Springer or heavy monkey climber (Fig.30). Although your visual indicator will drop a little due to line stretch, this should not be more than one inch (2.5cm). If it drops more, it does so because your line wasn't tight enough in the first place! Any takes at long range will probably be a single bleep followed by a drop back or screamer as the carp panics and draws the hook home on the tight line.

5. The use of backleads – as we detailed in the piece on slack lining, there are waters where the carp are wary of tight lines and you need to think your way around the problem. Whilst slack lining is one way round it, backleading also has its advantages. Backleading as the name suggests is the use of a second lead behind the end tackle to hold the mainline

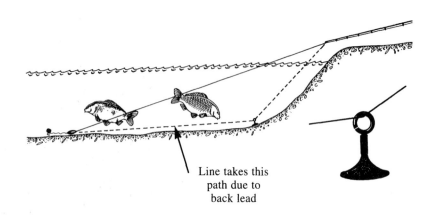

Line takes this
path due to
back lead

Fig. 31. Back leading

tight to the lake bed and out of harm's way. As the diagram illustrates
(Fig.31), this solves the problem of mid-water lines and unlike slack lining allows you to keep a fairly tight line between rod tip and end tackle. This can be essential when you are fishing near snags and weed and
want an indication as soon as possible. Unfortunately, backleads are not
100% foolproof as they do occasionally have a tendency to snag up
when playing fish so be careful on snaggy type waters. However, providing you use them correctly and to your advantage, they are an essential item in your tackle box. As an alternative to the conventional clip-
on back lead, you can use the Carp 'R' Us Flyback Tungsten tube which
is threaded onto the main line when tackling up. It is stopped at the
required position by a float stop or Powergum stop knot on the main
line. This system is less likely to catch on snags and weed and is particularly good when you require a back lead not too far from your terminal
tackle. Whether you do use a backlead or slack line remember that at
over 30 yards' (27m) range most of the mainline will be on the lake bed
anyway, unless you are fishing high rods and very tight lines. So if you
are fishing at that range or further out and merely want to avoid carp
coming into contact with the mainline in the vicinity of the baited area,
don't worry – it will be anyway and you don't need to adopt any specialist tactics.

6. Hookbait Types and Preparation Ideas

One thing that all carp rigs have in common is that they all possess a hookbait of one form or other. Things have progressed dramatically since the days of using exactly the same hookbait as free offerings and hookbaits are now a science in their own right. From balanced pop-ups to glugged bottom baits, it can all be very confusing and unfortunately if you get the hookbait side of things wrong it is possible to ruin what would otherwise be an excellent rig. You cannot just stick any old hookbait on your rig and hope it will work – many times it won't. A little forward thinking, some preparation at home and some fine tuning will produce dividends and makes correct hookbait thinking just as important as any other factor involved in carp rigs.

BASIC TYPES OF HOOKBAITS

Bottom Bait
Balanced Bait
Pop-Up Bait

BOTTOM BAIT

Standard bottom baits which mirror your free offerings are the commonest form of hookbait used on many waters today and are very effective.

a) Bottom Baits from Readymades – to use a readymade as a bottom bait is simple. Simply take one out of the packet and put it on your hook or hair rig. If you wish to make it a little smaller than your free offerings you can trim it down with a craft knife. To make it larger simply use a larger readymade than your free offerings.
b) Bottom Baits from Base Mixes – simply make your mix up as usual and make a number of extra baits to use on the rig. It is a good idea to make some smaller or larger than you intend your free offerings to be.

Big 20 taken using a stiffened pop-up rig.

BALANCED BAIT

To achieve a degree of buoyancy in your hookbait you can incorporate a pop-up into it which in turn will produce a balanced bait. The purpose of a balanced bait is to negate the weight of the hook and hooklength so that when it is cast into the water it slowly sinks. This buoyancy can act as a way of fooling carp in that it will be more buoyant than standard bottom baits or freebaits; when the carp sucks the bait in, it may not notice the potential danger and the balanced bait will be taken well into the carp's mouth, thus aiding hooking. If carp have wised up to standard bottom baits this can provide you with an advantage over conventional tactics. When balancing a bait you can balance it so it sinks very gradually or you can make it sink a little quicker but still be lighter than a standard bottom bait or freebie.

a) Balanced Baits from Readymades – to make a balanced bait from a readymade you have to add buoyancy to it. Obviously, if you are lucky enough to have chosen a readymade from a firm which also sells pop-ups in exactly the same flavour it's already done for you. All you need to do is purchase some readymade pop-ups in the sizes you want and use putty to balance them. Firms such as Kevin Maddocks and Mainline do sell readymade pop-ups. However, if you are using a readymade boily which doesn't have a pop-up to match you will have to use a neutral (no flavour) pop-up from the Kevin Maddocks range which can be sprayed or glugged with flavour or, one of the following methods:-

   1. Microwave or fry or bake the standard freebie to produce a pop-up. This is very hit and miss and we wouldn't recommend it at all due to the fact that the pop-up produced will be very much different from the standard freebie.
   2. Take a standard protein mix and add the flavour and colour to that pro-tein mix and make a polyballed pop-up to match the standard freebie.

b) Balanced Baits from Base Mixes – many people do indeed prefer to make their own baits so it is vital that you learn how to make balanced baits from those mixes.

   1. Once you've made your paste as normal you break a piece off and roll it between thumb and first finger.
   2. Next, using either $\frac{1}{4}$ inch (6mm) or $\frac{1}{2}$ inch (12mm) polyball, wrap the paste round the polyball so that it covers it as the diagram illustrates (Fig.32). Generally, an outer surround of one eigth of an inch (3mm) is ideal.
   3. Roll the coated polyballs round in your palm to ensure they are equal-ly coated and well shaped.
   4. Place the polyballed baits in boiling water for the required period and keep turning them to ensure all the skin is boiled.

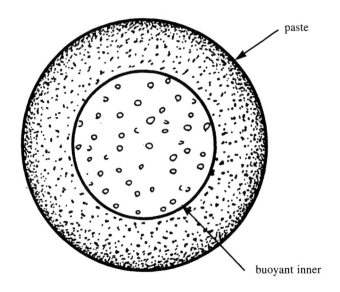

Fig. 32. Coated Polyball

5. Take the baits from the water and place them on an absorbent piece of cloth. Once they are on the cloth, keep moving them around to make sure all of the bait is dry and no moist areas remain.
6. Leave the baits on a separate piece of cloth to dry overnight. Freeze and use as needed.

POP-UPS

These are very popular and useful because they allow you to present a bait off the bottom so that it can easily be found by the carp and is less likely to get caught up in weed. Normal pop-ups are made by incorporating a polyball into your paste before boiling and you can make them as buoyant as you wish, depending on the size of the polyball used and outer surround of paste (Fig.33). Pop-ups catch large numbers of carp each year but because they are very different from freebaits and effective as carp catchers, the carp can eventually wise up to standard pop-up presentations.

a) Pop-Ups from Readymade Baits – this mirrors exactly that which produces balanced baits as we detailed earlier. Either purchase a readymade pop-up or use either of the two other techniques we detailed.
b) Pop-Ups from Base Mixes – again this mirrors what we said about making balanced baits. However, with a pop-up you should make it as buoy-

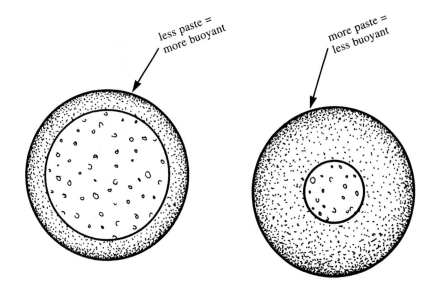

Fig. 33. Polyball size?

ant as possible so use less outer surround paste and more buoyancy insert.

PASTE HOOKBAITS?

You don't actually have to use boiled baits as hookbaits as it's perfectly acceptable to use paste as a hookbait. Clearly the paste will have to be firm enough to withstand casting, to stay on the hook when in the water and to withstand the attentions of the other species. The advantage of paste is that the attractors leak out almost instantly and once the carp takes in the hook and hookbait the paste will come off, so making it far more likely that the hook will catch hold. You can mould the paste round the hook or if you prefer to use a hair rig mould it round the matchstick as the diagram illustrates (Fig.34). For winter fishing or short session angling, paste hookbaits are an excellent edge.

CONSIDERATIONS TO BEAR IN MIND FOR ALL HOOKBAITS

Size
Shape
Colour
Texture

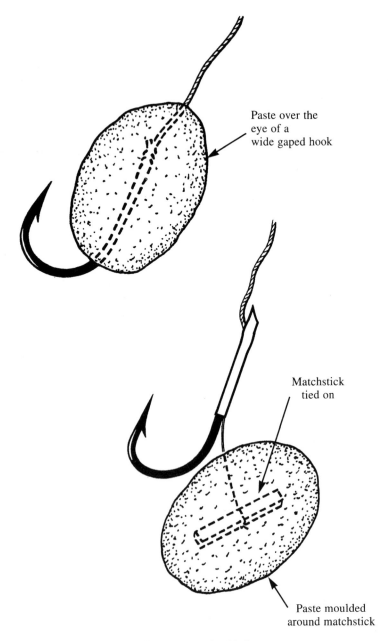

Paste over the
eye of a
wide gaped hook

Matchstick
tied on

Paste moulded
around matchstick

Fig. 34. Paste hookbaits

SIZE

Generally we advocate the use of 14–16 mm baits but there is no limit as far as size goes. As a general rule of thumb try to use the smallest size of boily you can. The smaller the bait the more the carp will eat before they encounter the one with the hook in, which can make them more confident in picking up baits. Also, with smaller baits you can put more out to the baited area without worrying about filling the carp up before the hookbait is encountered. One pound (450g) of base mix will make about 250 × 14 mm boilies or 80 × 20 mm baits. A spread of that many 14 mm baits is far more likely to keep the carp in your swim than the 20 mm ones, providing you can reach the baited area with those smaller baits. Clearly, your hookbait would usually match the size of your free offering but there is nothing to stop you using a larger or smaller hookbait. This could well catch the carp out and is always worth trying in that it's different!

SHAPE

Most anglers tend to use round baits, though there is no rule which says you have to. Round baits are commonly used because that's the way ready-mades are manufactured and common usage becomes accepted usage. If you are fishing at over 30 yards or so, you may need to use round boilies to be accurate with your baiting up. Baits which are misshaped and fly all over the place can end up as wasted baits and if those freebaits don't draw the carp to your hookbait, they may take the carp away from it. By making your hookbait a different shape from the normal round ones that many anglers use, you can catch the carp out in two fairly distinctive ways. Firstly, the carp will have seen round baits time and time again and by being different (i.e. using a different shape) you could surprise the carp. Secondly, an odd shaped hookbait will be harder for the carp to eject than a perfectly round one. Edges cause a bait to jar and bounce in the mouth which can in turn lead to an increased likelihood of the hook finding a home.

COLOUR

This, too, can make a difference to success, especially when you are fishing fairly shallow waters or fishing your bait to shallower areas in a lake. How carp view certain colours has yet to be totally proved, though they certainly can distinguish between what shows up dark or light in the water. Bright colours can provide quite a contrast over weed or mud and it is possibly the contrast of colours that the carp pick up on. Certainly, in water under 13 feet which is not overcoloured the carp can pick up these brighter colours in anything other than low light conditions. Whatever your views on that one, it is fair to say that some waters respond best to bright baits and some to darker coloured ones. When brightly coloured baits were in vogue and the carp had been pressurised on them, these baits were viewed with suspicion by some carp on some waters and using darker coloured bait could prove an advantage. However, on many waters, due to the popularity of fishmeal baits, reddy-brown seems to be the predominant colour used, so a bright coloured bait may produce dividends. Why not try a different coloured hookbait from your free offerings colour? It could produce results. Why not even try a different kind of free offering as well? All this can take the carp by surprise which is what you are trying to do on many waters today. However, always appreciate that carp will not be able to see the boilies it is feeding on at night or in coloured or deep water.

TEXTURE

Most baits seem to feel exactly the same and if you possibly can, try to vary your hookbait so it has a different texture from the other baits. You can add various ingredients such as seeds when making your hookbaits and this can produce a hookbait with a different texture from the free offerings. Boiling the hookbait longer or shorter than normal can also do this. A long boil would make your hookbait hard so that the carp has to take it well back to crush it. This could make it hard for the carp to reject it and once that hooklength tightens up the hook should prick home. By boiling the bait for a shorter than normal period it will be a lot softer and will crumble or crush in the carp's mouth which will leave the hook free to find a hookhold rather than being ejected along with the hookbait. This can make a difference.

OVERFLAVOURED HOOKBAITS

In order to catch carp you have to persuade the carp to take the hookbait into its mouth and to do that you have to make your hookbait attractive. If your hookbait is exactly the same as the 300 freebaits or whatever it's resting in, your chance of a pick-up is 300 – 1, all things being equal. However, if your hookbait is more attractive than those freebaits, your chances of a pick-up should increase. You can increase the hookbait's chance of being taken by making it a pop-up or adding a stringer, but another way is by using an overflavoured hookbait. By boosting the attraction level of your hookbait your chances can increase considerably, in our experience, especially in the winter. On some waters the carp may well be wary of stronger smelling hookbaits but on most waters this is worth trying.

a) How to produce an overflavoured hookbait from base mixes

   1. Generally, when we talk about overflavouring hookbaits we are talking about doubling the flavour level of the type of hookbait in question.

With a good blow on the water the carp may feed strongly.

2. In that case, if you are using, say, 5ml of flavour and 6 drops of essential oil in your six egg mix, to achieve a double flavour hookbait all you do is use the same amount of attractors in half as many eggs. In the above example you would use 5ml of flavour and 6 drops of essential oil in a three egg mix.

3. Next, add your choice of base mix to the liquid part of the mix and make up your paste as you would normally. Because you are using only three eggs but the same level of attractors, the paste that is produced will be double strength.

4. Make your bottom bait, pop-up or whatever. Freeze and use as needed.

Please note that this double flavouring of bait is only to be used with hookbaits and must not be used to produce normal freebaits. Because the carp will not get to digest the overflavoured bait it will not put it off and cannot do the fish any harm, but if it were to eat overflavoured freebaits it would almost certainly put it off the feed and might suffer. At worst, it would not seek that source of attraction again and at best it would not go near the baited area at all.

b) How to produce an overflavoured bait from readymades

Strictly speaking it is impossible to produce an overflavoured hookbait from readymades unless you wish to add neat flavours or other attractors to the readymade hookbaits when you've purchased them. To overflavour readymades you can soak the hookbaits in a small amount of flavour, or hookbait soak, or you can follow the technique we used to produce a pop-up. Simply use a conventional milk protein base mix, three eggs and normal flavour level (5ml or whatever) and make an overflavoured bottom bait or pop-up. This is another excellent method and one we would advise you to choose. Kevin Maddocks produces a range of Hookbait Enhancers which are perfect for producing overflavoured hookbaits.

BAIT SOAKS

A bait soak is a solution of liquids such as fish oils, vegetable oils, aminos etc. Pour these bulk liquids into an empty freezer bag, add your hookbaits to them, let the liquids soak into them once you've shaken them thoroughly and use after the baits have had 2–4 hours of soaking. You can even add a limited amount of concentrated flavour to these soaks to give them your own individual label. Once catapulted out into the water, these bulk liquids leak out from the hookbaits, giving a homing signal for the carp to increase your chances of a pick-up.

GLUGGING OF BAITS

Very similar to bait soaks, glugging of bait is adding liquids to your already boiled baits to draw the carps' attention to the food. Not all carp swim inches from the bottom and by using glugged hookbaits you can create a feeding trail to carp swimming at all levels in the water. Because many oils float, any baits soaked in such oils will leak out oils which will make their way to the surface of the lake. As the carp swim into this trail of oil they will hopefully follow it down to its source and find the hookbaits. It is an excellent idea and one which when used sensibly is very effective indeed. Here's how to glug baits.

1. Put 20–30 ml of oil into a strong freezer bag. You can also add neat flavour to the oil.
2. Add your hookbaits to this oiled bag.
3. Inflate the bag, seal it and shake well to ensure even distribution of the oils.
4. Allow the oil 4–12 hours to soak into the baits.

A glugged bait will leak oil for up to 12 hours and as the baits are attacked by nuisance fish and/or carp, more oil will be given off, hopefully inciting the carp into feeding.

Many major firms such as Kevin Maddocks, Nutrabaits and Richworth sell bait dips, soaks etc, formulated specifically for your hookbait. The concentration levels in the tubs or sprays have been precisely formulated so it is a good idea to use them if you wish to increase the potency of your hookbait this way.

NUISANCE SPECIES

Of course, not only carp are attracted to your hookbaits and you will inevitably find that on some waters you will encounter nuisance species attacking your hookbaits. It could be limited to very small roach or at the other end of the spectrum it could be the deadly crayfish. A hookbait is only effective as such when it is still there for the carp to pick up. If it's come off the hook/hair, if it's been nibbled away, you are wasting your time and your rig is ineffective. Always be aware of the nuisance species in your water and tailor your hookbait preparation accordingly. Normally by making your hookbait harder will deter nuisance fish but you have to balance that to losing its attractiveness due to excess boiling etc. Also, with some species like the crayfish, standard hookbaits are a waste of time and no matter how long you boil them the crayfish will rip them to shreds. In such cases you have to use air dried baits which are rock hard or choose a ready made, such as the KM range, which are very hard and will resist the attentions of other species and crayfish. Think about what you are doing when preparing and using a hookbait and you will enjoy more success in the long run.

Frosty 20 taken after accurate plumbing found the hotspot.

7. End Tackles

There are many different types of end tackles available for carp fishing and to list each and every one would be impossible in a book of this nature. For that reason we've restricted our coverage of end tackles to the proven ones. To a large extent all the end tackles we shall detail now include the same components just in different ways. To construct an end tackle you will need to possess some or all of the following items:-

Mainline – Anti-tangle tubing – Swivels – Beads – Lead core fly line – Incidental tubing – Shockleader material – Snagleader material – Leads

Now let's cover some factors involved in end tackles before we detail the recommended ones we'd advise you to use.

LEADS

For all the end tackles you will need to use a lead weight and we'd advise you to choose a Korda, M.C.F., Carp 'R' Us Profile or Streamselect one. However, it's not just a case of any lead will do, and when we cover precise end tackles you will see that certain situations demand certain leads. Two points should be covered now.

COATING YOUR LEAD?

Because your hookbait invariably ends up next to your lead, due to it dropping down the same arc made by the lead (Fig.35) there is a great deal to be said in favour of making your leads match the lake bed. While on many waters it may not make a difference to your catch rates, on some pressurised waters or shallow clear waters where a black lead over sand or mud or gravel will stand out, it can make a difference. Even if that difference is only a few fish a year it has to be worth the effort.

You can actually buy some leads ready coated in a limited range of colours, but as many lakes have different coloured lake beds it is worth while coating your leads to match your lake bed. You can purchase powder to do this from most major tackle shops but a far easier way is as follows:-

71

Fig. 35. Hookbait usually ends up next to lead

1. Make sure your lead is smooth to the touch and clean.
2. Using Airfix or Humbrol model paints, paint it to the required shade to match your lake bed. This could be one single colour or a camouflaged effect. Allow the paint to set overnight.
3. Take a tube of Kryston Hawser and squeeze a blob of it on to your coloured lead. Then using either a brush or your fingers, smear the Hawser all over the lead so it's evenly coated. Allow six hours to harden and then do it again to make sure it's fully coated and smooth to the touch. Allow twenty-four hours to harden fully.
4. Soak the coated leads in a bucket of water overnight and they are then ready for use.

This is almost as good as your conventional coating process, is more exact colour-wise and protects your leads from gravel bar damage.

SIZE OF LEAD?

Generally we expect a lead to self-hook a carp but there are certain circumstances where you will use what is known as a confidence set-up. If you are using a lead to self-hook carp and make the carp drag the hook in and bolt off in panic, you should use the heaviest lead you can safely use in all the circumstances. Usually this will be $2\frac{1}{2}$–4 oz (70-115g). If you want to use a confidence set-up use a light lead and if it's a bolt effect you want, use a heavier one. Don't get those principles mixed up and start using 1 oz (30g) bolt leads and 4 oz (115g) confidence ones.

IN-LINE OR HELICOPTER DESIGN?

Whether the end tackle you decide to use incorporates anti-tangle tubing or not you will have to decide whether to use an in-line set-up or helicopter set-up. With an in-line set-up your lead is mounted directly on your mainline and you are pulling at the swivel to which the hooklink is attached. With a helicopter type set-up your lead is tied to your mainline and you are pulling at the lead, not the hooklength swivel (Fig.36). On clear, open waters this does not really matter but when fishing in weed or near snags, it can matter a great deal. When fishing to weedy areas it's vital to have a direct line of pull on the carp, and if the carp is pulling at the swivel and you at the lead you don't have that. This can cause all sorts of problems. By using the in-line leads you can get a direct pull at the carp and so control its fight for freedom. While in-line leads do not cast quite as well as their helicopter counterparts we'd urge you to use them on all but the most open of waters.

RUNNING LEAD OR FIXED LEAD?

Although many end tackles utilise a semi-fixed lead it is a good idea to experiment with running leads as well (Fig.37). With a running lead the carp is free to take line until you strike into the fish or it feels the resistance of a line clip or whatever. If you do decide to use a running lead don't make the mistake of using a light lead to cut down on resistance. It's a nice thought but in reality it doesn't work. A light lead will not resist the pulling motion that a taking carp creates and it will drag the lead as well thus creating an extra and sometimes uneven resistance which could easily cause the carp to eject the bait. By using a heavier lead such as 2 oz (60g) or more this movement is resisted and the line is able to move freely. With the running lead set-up use a large bore low resistance leger ring to attach the lead to the line. This allows the line to be taken easier. With running leads you should not encounter drop backs as whatever way the carp moves it will be taking line. If you do encounter drop backs it may be that your lead is too light or the line is not running freely. Running leads can be fished with or without tubing or with lead core line dependant on the nature of the lake bed you are fishing on. Normally a tubeless end tackle utilising a running lead is used but you may wish to change that, and possibly include a shockleader or snagleader into the end tackle. Wary carp feed with great caution and often move very little with the bait – in this case a fixed lead will help ensure that the carp pricks itself, but this will only happen if all the other features of the rig are correct at that time. It is also worth considering the Carp 'R' Us Startle Rig system – this permits

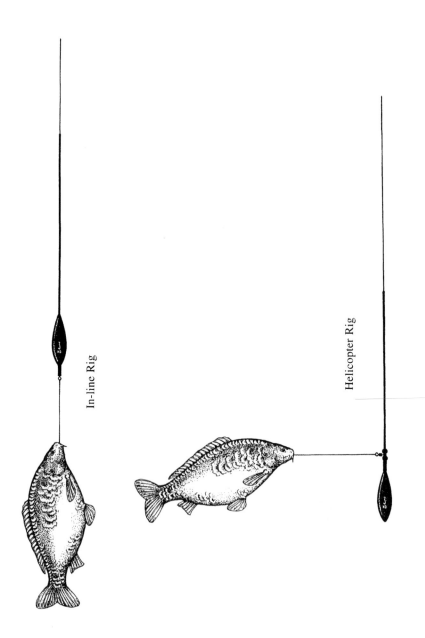

Fig. 36. In-line -v- Helicopter design

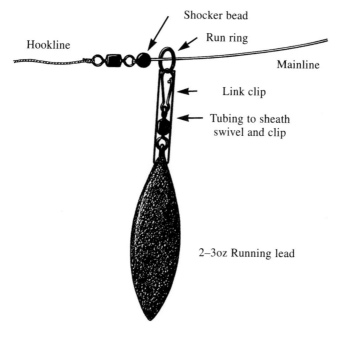

Fig. 37(a). Running lead set-up

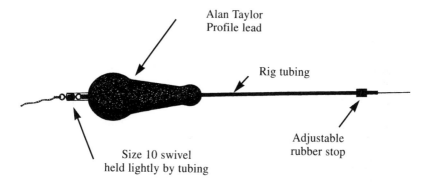

Fig. 37(b). Carp 'R' Us Startle Rig

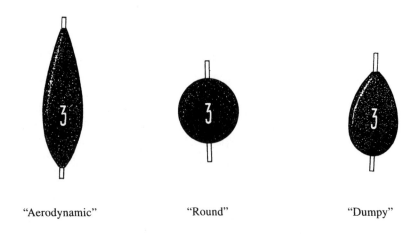

"Aerodynamic"   "Round"   "Dumpy"

Fig. 38. Lead shapes

you to use either a fixed lead or running lead with an adjustable backstop without dismantling the system (see Fig. 37b).

LEAD SHAPES?

There are various designs and shapes of leads available (Fig.38). The less aerodynamic a lead is the more resistance it will create to a carp which has tightened the hooklink against the lead as it will at first only feel the narrow end of the lead. In silt or weed a standard aerodynamic lead will suffice in that the nature of the lake bed accentuates the weight of the lead. However, if you are fishing on hard gravel you will need to use a dumpy or round lead to increase that resistance. Look at the situation you find yourself in and whether you need to make that lead as heavy as possible.

ATTRACTA LEADS

Streamselect manufacture a special design of lead called an Attracta lead which is very useful in the right circumstances. The grooves in the lead allow you to add capsules into which you can inject neat flavour. Using a syringe, you inject the flavour into the capsules, secure the capsules with the elastic band and cast out to the desired spot. Once in the water the capsules dissolve, the neat flavour leaks out and provides a feeding signal to passing or localized carp. Because the flavour is in a liquid form it has all the attraction of a number of baits, but the only bait for the carp to pick up is the one with the hook in it. In winter this can be a brilliant idea as

30 plus on a very basic end tackle.

you don't have to worry about the carp filling themselves up on freebaits at the expense of a take on your baited hook. You don't actually have to use neat flavour as you can use fish oils, milk, cream or whatever you wish to in order to draw the carp to the hookbait. Always be very careful with the syringe and keep plenty of capsules handy for regular recasting in winter. Attracta leads are now available in both in-line and helicopter designs so you can use them in all situations.

ANTI-TANGLE TUBING

All anglers dread tangles because a tangle can negate the effect of a successful bait in the right place at the right time or cause a tackle failure when playing a fish. No matter how hard you've worked at getting all the variables right, if the rig is tangled and the hookbait can't be picked up, you are wasting your time. Tangles occur when in mid-air your hook-length, hair and hook wrap round your mainline and knot. To avoid this, anti-tangle tubing was developed which sheaths your mainline. While nothing is completely tangle-proof, anti-tangle tubing does help tremendously. One of the big disadvantages of rig tubing is that air can get trapped inside and lift the tubing off the bottom thereby spooking the carp. When this occurs you need to use one of the balancing aids detailed earlier.

END TACKLES WITHOUT ANTI-TANGLE TUBING

On some waters the carp may well be wary of tubing and to keep one step ahead of them it's necessary to use tubeless end tackles. Although it doesn't happen on all waters, on shallow, clear and pressurised waters the carp can wise up to tubing and it's best to try to avoid its use if you can. However, unless you are fishing at very short range and can see the end tackle and presentation drop in untangled, or you are using nylon hook-links, there is always the danger of a mid-flight tangle. To avoid tangles without using tubing all you need to do is add a stringer to your hook. The effect of a stringer is to bounce the presentation off your mainline and this works very well. You don't actually need to use a multi-bait stringer as a two-bait one will do it perfectly. You can also use Kryston's Superstiff gel which hardens hooklengths when you cast them out, but once in water dissolves leaving your hooklength as supple as it ever was. Lead core fly line also can cut down on tangles due to its rigidity.

SHOCKLEADERS

If you are fishing at range you will need a shockleader to absorb the force of the cast. When tying up an end tackle which uses a shockleader you must ensure that all the components of the end tackle can pass over the shockleader knot if your mainline breaks. Be it a confidence, in-line or helicopter rig fished on a shockleader if any of those components cannot pass over the knot it can be a death or tether rig. So ensure all the components have a large central bore and that your shockleader knot is neat and tidy. Always think of the carp and what could happen if your mainline breaks.

LEAD CORE FLY LINE

Because lead core fly line lies flat against the lake bed it is a very advantageous product to use when used in shallow clear water or when the carp are wary or spooky of conventional end tackles. As with what we said about shockleaders, your components in the end tackle must be able to pass over the lead core knot in the event of a breakage.

End Tackle No.1
    Helicopter Rig With Tubing (Fig.39)

End Tackle No.2
    Helicopter Rig Without Tubing (Fig.40)

End Tackle No.3
    Helicopter Rig With Lead Core Fly Line (Fig.41)

End Tackle No.4
    In-Line Rig With Tubing (Fig.42)

End Tackle No.5
    In-Line Rig Without Tubing (Fig.43)

End Tackle No.6
    In-Line Rig With Lead Core Fly Line (Fig.44)

End Tackle No.7
    Confidence Rigs With Tubing (Fig.45)

End Tackle No.8
    Confidence Rig Without Tubing (Fig.46)

End Tackle No.9
    Confidence Rig With Lead Core Fly Line (Fig.47)

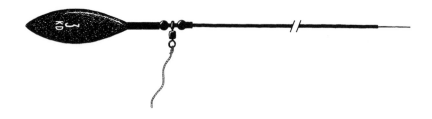

Fig. 39. Helicopter Rig with tubing

Fig. 40. Helicopter Rig without tubing

Needle knot

Fig. 41. Helicopter Rig with lead core flyline

Fig. 42. In-line Rig with tubing

Fig. 43. In-line Rig without tubing

Needle knot

Fig. 44. In-line Rig with lead core fly line

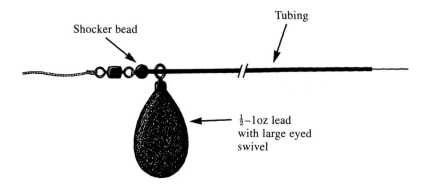

Fig. 45. Confidence Rig with tubing

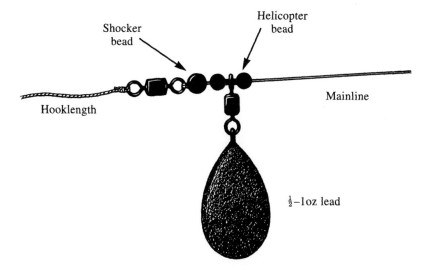

Fig. 46. Confidence Rig without tubing

Fig. 47. Confidence Rig with lead core fly line

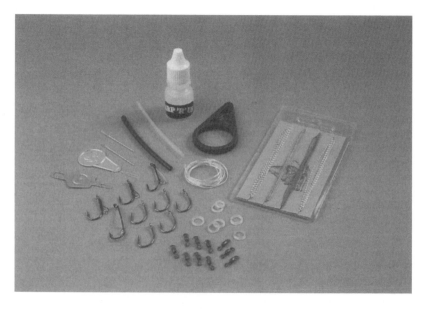

The Carp 'R' Us rig making kit comes complete with
comprehensive instructions.

8. *Presentations*

Along with end tackles, carp rig presentations have become very confused. For that reason we have restricted this chapter to only those presentations which have a proven track record. You may not need to use all these presentations but be aware of them so that you are able to cope with any situation you may find yourself presented with. Although we will cover all the presentations you need we do not cover any we feel are dangerous to the carp and could result in foul hooking or a tethered fish. This is unacceptable.

THE QUESTION OF PRESENTATION?

Having decided which end tackle is best suited to the water and swim you are fishing, your next choice is to decide which presentation to use. Combining your end tackle and presentation will give you the finished carp rig.

STANDARD BOTTOM BAIT (Fig. 48)

Providing your water isn't too weedy, a bottom bait can be a very effective way of catching carp. As you can see, the bottom bait is fished on a hair and hangs as pictured. For most situations this is fine. A line aligner generally improves the presentation and if possible we would advise you to use a stringer to amplify the attraction of the hookbait. Always try to balance your hook size to the bait size as too large a hook for the size of bait can lead to the hookbait being identified as dangerous. Alternatively, too small a hook for the size of bait can cause the presentation not to self-hook as the bait may bounce the hook out. To vary your presentation, shorten or lengthen the hooklength or hairlength and vary the size of bait and hook.

BALANCED BOTTOM BAIT (Fig. 49)

By utilising a buoyant bait as the hookbait you can achieve a balanced bait presentation. Use just the right size of bait to sink the hooklength slowly or, alternatively, add a little putty or liquid weight round the eye of the hook to sink it. Because this "slow sink" process is vital to its effect, don't

Fig. 48. Standard bottom bait

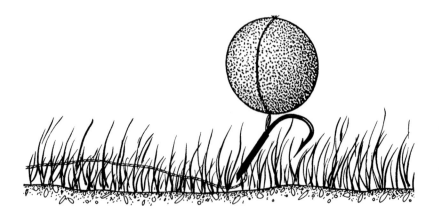

Fig. 49. Balanced bottom bait

add a stringer to the hook as it might drag it into the weed or silt. This presentation can be used on all lake bottoms but it is particularly effective over light bottom weed. You can use it on a semi-fixed end tackle or confidence end tackle but use liquid weight or putty to stop the looping effect which can occur with it. While 12 inches (30cm) is a good starting point for length of your hooklength, try varying it up to 24 inches (60cm) or more at times.

DOUBLE BOTTOM BAIT (Fig. 50)

When the carp are feeding strongly on your bait, or if you want to draw attention to it, a double bottom bait is very effective. Always use a wide-gape hook for increased likelihood of self-hooking and don't make your hair too long or it will wrap back on itself and could tangle. Although this presentation is best used on weed-free bottoms by incorporating a buoyant bait as one of the two used (usually the one furthest from the hook), you can negate the weight effect of the other bait, hook, and so on. Normally it is fished on a short hooklength of 5–10 inches (13–25cm) but if you are using a buoyant bait you can increase that to 16 inches (40cm) or more. On clear bottoms by all means add a stringer to amplify the attraction level and make it harder to reject.

Fig. 50. Double bottom bait

A double 20mm "Snowman" presented on a 15 pounds nylon hooklink
proved the downfall of this 46–10.

Fig. 51. Multiple Bait Rig

MULTIPLE BAIT RIG (Fig. 51)

By incorporating three or more baits on your hair you can create a multiple bait presentation. Because of the nature of this presentation, once taken in by a carp it is difficult to reject and generally the smaller the baits the more effective it is. You can either use a dental floss hair or continue the braid to mount the baits on. Short hooklengths work particularly well with this form of presentation and by incorporating one buoyant bait into the row of baits you can achieve a "slow sink" effect. This presentation is very effective in silt as it's particularly hard for the carp to eject. Do not use a stringer with it or you may find the carp have difficulty taking it all in cleanly.

ANCHOR RIG (Fig. 52)

Whilst the line aligner presentation for bottom baits is very effective, it does not always result in a hook finding a hold in the carp's mouth. To improve the efficiency of the line aligner you can turn it into an anchor rig. The bristle going through the line aligner stops the hook sliding out of the carp's mouth and it causes the hook to turn or jar in far more often. Looking very similar to a ship's anchor in design it is an improvement on

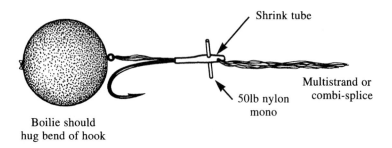

Shrink tube

Multistrand or
combi-splice

50lb nylon
mono

Boilie should
hug bend of hook

Fig. 52. Anchor Rig

Multistrand or
combi-splice

Fig. 53. The Cranked Hook set-up

the line aligner and for presenting bottom baits in silt or on gravel it's an excellent aid to hooking carp. You can purchase Carp 'R' Us ready tied hooks/hooklengths with the anchor inbuilt or by using stiff nylon, bristles or fuse wire you can duplicate it. Pierce the shrink tube before boiling, push the bristle through it and add steam to the shrink tube to hold it securely. A little drop of superglue can be used for added security.

CRANKED HOOK RIG (Fig. 53)

Although there are a number of different designs of hooks available most are very similar. The cranked hook is quite a radical hook as can be seen. The various bends in it cause it to flip over and sometimes find a hookhold with greater efficiency than a standard line aligner. Although it may look similar to a bent hook it's more effective and causes less damage to the carp's mouth. The cranked hook rig can be used for bottom baits or pop-ups and although it's a lot stronger than it looks it should not be used in thick weed or tight to snags. Cranked hooks can be made by bending long shanked lure hooks as illustrated or you can purchase them ready cranked from the Carp 'R' Us range.

COMBI-LINK (Fig. 54)

On pressurised waters you may need to make your presentation as subtle as possible and this is where the combi-link comes into its own. Due to its fine multistrand make-up, once immersed in water it will give the hookbait a high degree of free movement. You can use it with either bottom baits or buoyant baits but if you do use a buoyant bait, make sure the hooklength does not loop up. While the presentation can be fished on standard semi-fixed leads it is at its most effective on a confidence type end tackle. We would not advise it to be used in weed or near snags but it is highly effective in gravel pits or in silt.

Fig. 54. Combi-Link

STANDARD POP-UP RIG (Fig. 55)

Pop-up presentations are very effective for hooking carp in that they allow the carp to find the hookbait easily and once taken, can be difficult to reject. This is particularly so over weed as you can present a bait over the weed. Normally fish the bait popped-up 1–3 inches (25–75mm) but you can increase this if the weed is particularly bad. Keep the actual hooklength as short as possible to aid self-hooking and you can either critically balance or overshot depending on the nature of the lake bed and methods the carp have been subjected to.

One of 4 × 20's in a day – the rig was spot on!

Fig. 55. Standard Pop-Up

CRITICALLY BALANCING (Fig. 56)

When you use a pop-up, unless you decide to have it popped-up direct from the lead, you will need to use some sort of balancing aid to hold it down at the required height from the lake bed. On waters which haven't seen this tactic before you can use whatever counterweight you want so that the pop-up sinks down to the prescribed level. However, because many waters have seen this tactic year in year out, critical balancing comes into use. With this process you use just enough counterweight that it counteracts the buoyancy of the pop-up and causes the presentation to sink down slowly and rest lightly on the lake bed. It is extremely useful for two main reasons. Firstly, because it sinks slowly it will rest on top of weed and will be easy for the carp to find. Secondly, when the carp sucks it in because of its fine point of balance it will fly into the carp's mouth and will be a little more difficult for the carp to get rid of. On many waters this is an excellent way to fool the carp.

OVERSHOTTING (Fig. 57)

Moving on one step further, if the carp have been caught time and time again on critically balanced baits they may well become a little wary of them and you will need to look towards another way of fishing your pop-

Fig. 56. Critically balancing

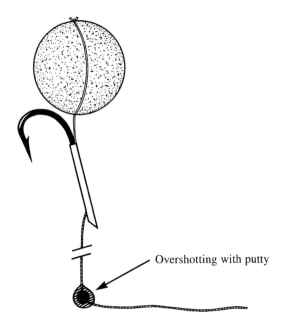

Overshotting with putty

Fig. 57. Overshotting

up. Critically balanced baits do waft about when the carp move in to feed so they can become identifiable and consequently may be treated with caution. By using more weight than is necessary to hold the pop-up down, commonly known as overbalancing, or overshotting, the carp may be fooled once again. This pop-up won't waft about yet will be in a position for the carp to take it in. Because the pop-up is overshotted, once pop-up and counterweight enter the carp's mouth they will be difficult to eject. On pressurised waters this is a good tactic to use.

SLIDING RING RIG (Fig. 58)

In order to make the hookbait and hook separate in the carp's mouth, all sorts of weird and wonderful ideas have been dreamed up and this is one of the best ones yet. Instead of attaching the hair directly to the hook it's attached to a Drennan ring which runs between two stops. It can be used with bottom baits or pop-ups but is particularly effective when used with the latter. To construct the rig push one float stop over the point and up to the eye, then the ring and finally another float stop. As an alternative to using float stops, you can create stops by using a drop of Kesmark's rig glue and then a drop of hardener. This type of stop will not move during heavy casts. If you use a small ring you should have no problems with the ring jamming on a float stop; if you use a larger one crush it a little so it is oval rather than round. Now tie a boily onto a hair and tie that to the Drennan ring. When the hook and hookbait are sucked in both go in together. Upon rejection, the hookbait will swivel round on the ring and travel down the hook shank, thereby momentarily leaving the hook behind and is less likely to drag the hook out. This helps tremendously where carp are sucking and blowing at baits. Another successful version of this rig is to incorporate shrink tubing, with putty or shot added immediately below the tubing which is best curved inwards to create a bent hook effect. This version has been the most successful rig ever at the notoriously difficult Withy Pool (see Fig.58c).

BENT HOOK (Fig. 59)

Unfortunately, the bent hook is banned on many waters today but as it is a proven tactic and is still allowed on some waters it needs to be included. Bent hooks have been used for well over fifteen years (Kevin Maddocks and Len Middleton used them in 1980) but they really came into fashion in the late eighties in conjunction with pop-ups. The bend in the shank causes the hook to flip over in the carp's mouth as the hook link tightens up which increases the chances of the hook finding a hold in the bottom lip. For wary fish which are mouthing at baits this is an excellent way to catch them and fished on a short hooklength and large lead it's very effective. Unfortunately this bending of the shank creates a weak spot and

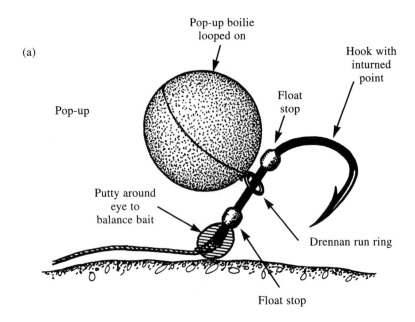

(a)

Pop-up boilie
looped on

Hook with
inturned
point

Float
stop

Pop-up

Putty around
eye to
balance bait

Drennan run ring

Float stop

(b)

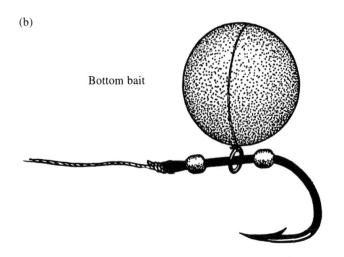

Bottom bait

Fig. 58(a,b). Sliding Ring Rig

(c)

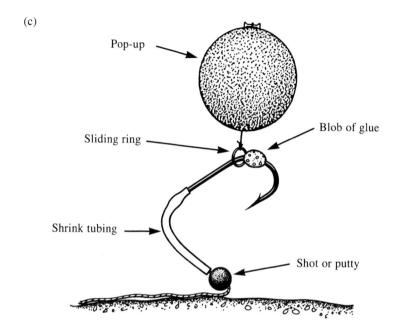

Pop-up

Sliding ring

Blob of glue

Shrink tubing

Shot or putty

Fig. 58(c). Withy Pool Sliding Ring Rig

under extreme pressure, say in weed or in snags, they have a tendency to open out or snap. Also because of the nature of the hook's design they have a tendency to wind and lever themselves in and twist during a fight which often creates mouth damage to the carp.

MEDUSA RIG (Fig. 60)

This is named after the Greek siren who had snakes for hair; can you see the resemblance with the maggots? All you do is superglue maggots all over the polyball and then use the polyball as you would a pop-up boily. Alternatively, you could use Kryston's Bogey to which the maggots will adhere. Use a long hair to ensure maximum separation between bait and hook once it's taken in and use a strong small hook.

LOONY EXTENSION RIG (Fig. 61)

This rig is so named because it was invented on the banks of Savay Lake by the "Loony Rota". This "Loony Rig" consists of a piece of stiff fine bored rig tubing about an inch and a half (40mm) in length wedged over

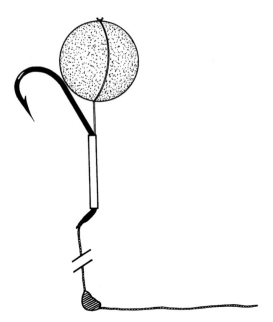

Fig. 59. Bent Hook

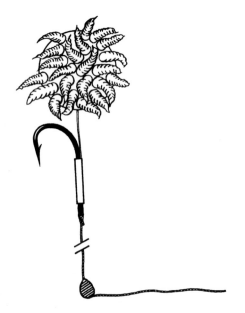

Fig. 60. Medusa Rig

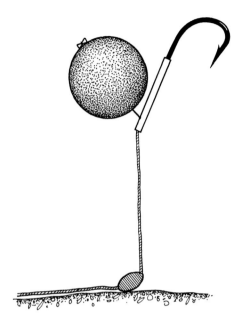

Fig. 61. Loony Extension Rig

the eye of the hook and the shank, making a stiff extension to the hook. To the base of the rig tubing, that being the furthest away from the bend of the hook, a very short hair mounted boily is attached. This is easiest done by making a hole with a fine needle through the rig tubing and attaching the hair. The hair will be no longer than about three eighths of an inch (9mm), ensuring that when the rig settles in the water the stiff tubing will hold the hook more or less upright with the boily lying alongside it, the top of the boily being about level with the eye of the hook.

THE SWIMMER RIG (Fig. 62)

Although the illustration is of a pop-up this can be used for bottom baits as well. On many waters this is an excellent presentation to use and should be fished critically balanced to allow it to "swim around" and get noticed whilst a fish is feeding close by. If you superglue the loop you will find it far easier to get the bait tight to the back of the hook so improving its efficiency. Alternatively, utilise the Carp 'R' Us Lightweight Swimmer Rig hook with bait band attachment.

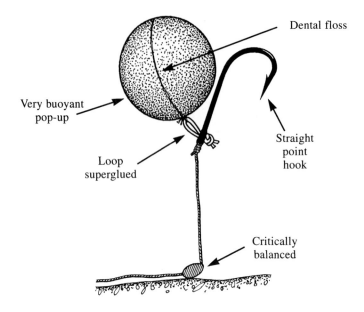

Dental floss

Very buoyant
pop-up

Loop
superglued

Straight
point
hook

Critically
balanced

Fig. 62. Swimmer Rig

CLAW RIG (Fig. 63)

Also known as weighted drop hook, this is quite radical and although it
looks a little unusual it can work very well indeed. This rig differs from
standard pop-up presentations in that the hair, for a change, points back up
the mainline and the counterbalance weight is on the hook not on the
hooklength. When the fish takes in the hook and hookbait the hook will
swirl in the carp's mouth and because the hook is weighted it will act as
a claw so clawing its way into the bottom lip of the carp. Once taken in
this is very difficult for the carp to reject which is a bonus on hard fished
waters today. This rig should only be used on gravel or silty bottoms. If
weed is present the claw will catch in the weed and the efficiency of the
rig will be reduced considerably.

BRISTLE RIG (Fig. 64)

This is not a new invention and even though very effective has yet to be
used on most waters today. By using either a bristle or very stiff monofilament such as Amnesia you are creating a reverse 'V' to the back of the
hook. The hook can be taken in as normal but when the carp seeks to eject
the hook the bristles will impede the clean exit out of the carp's mouth.
The force of ejection tends to split the bristles apart so making ejection
even more unlikely. This may well sound very complicated indeed but it is

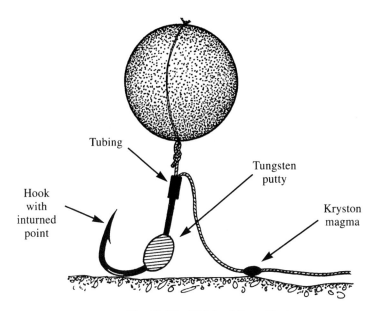

Tubing

Tungsten
putty

Hook
with
inturned
point

Kryston
magma

Fig. 63. The Weighted Drop Hook

highly effective. You can fish single or double bristles and although it can
be used with bottom baits, it is best suited to pop-up presentations.

BIG HOOK RIG (Fig. 65)

This is a very effective presentation where carp are pressurised and are
clamping their mouths close to the hookbait in order to test it. By using a
large hook it is very difficult for the carp to eject it and coupling a razor
sharp hook with a large lead makes the presentation a good alternative
when the carp have become wary of standard presentations. A large
cranked sea hook has a tendency to pivot round like a bent hook and
embed itself in the carp's bottom lip. This should always be used with pop-
ups and because of the weight of the hook you need to use a very buoyant
pop-up. Too large a pop-up would detract from the rig's effect so use small
microwaved pop-ups mounted on the run ring. The hook needs to be razor
sharp and should be either critically balanced or overshotted on a very
short hooklink. It is also effective when used in weed or silt where carp
have a tendency to mouth baits.

D-RIG (Fig. 66)

Where carp are sucking and blowing at hookbaits, it is usually essential to
make the hookbait and hook come apart as far as possible to aid self-

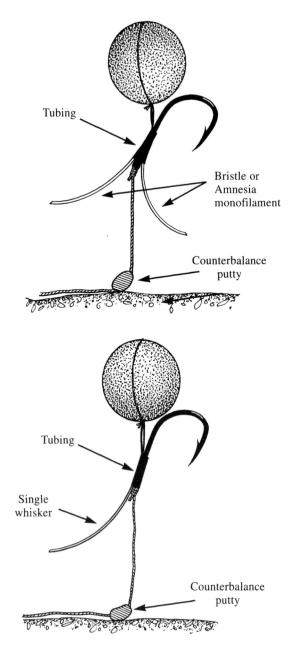

Fig. 64. Bristle Rigs

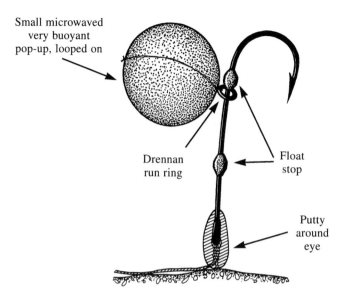

Small microwaved
very buoyant
pop-up, looped on

Drennan
run ring

Float
stop

Putty
around
eye

Fig. 65. Big Hook Rig

(a)

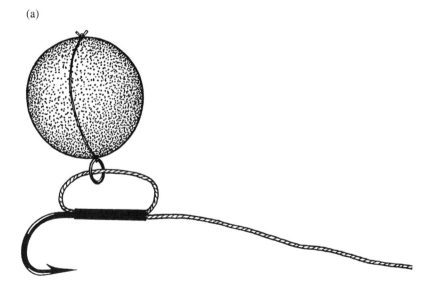

Fig. 66(a). D-Rig

(b)

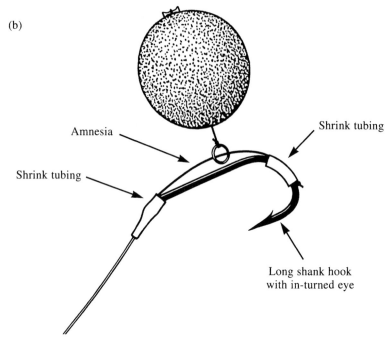

Amnesia

Shrink tubing

Shrink tubing

Long shank hook
with in-turned eye

Fig. 66(b). Amnesia D-Rig

hooking. With the D-rig, if the carp sucks the bait in and then seeks to
blow it out, the bait will go out first but due to the D-loop the hook may
well be delayed and blown into the carp's mouth. Alternatively, if the carp
picks the bait up and moves off, the hook will drag into the mouth.
Because the hook and hookbait are some distance apart, this is best used
in weed-free situations and although it can be used for a buoyant bait, it
is best suited to bottom baits. If used in silt, add a stringer to make it
harder to eject and because you are looking for the carp to drag the hook
into itself, use the smallest, lightest and sharpest hook you can use in all
the circumstances. There is another version of this rig-apart from using
braid for the D-loop you can use Amnesia or a very heavy nylon. This is
tied to the eye and the other end, which has an overhand knot tied in it, is
held in place by a short piece of shrink tubing (see Fig.66b). Alternatively,
Carp 'R' Us market a purposely designed Amnesia 'D' rig hook which
comes complete with D-loop and sliding ring.

POPPED-UP OFF THE LEAD (Fig. 67)

Generally, this presentation has very limited use but in the right circumstances it can be deadly. In silt, fish it on a short hooklength and once the

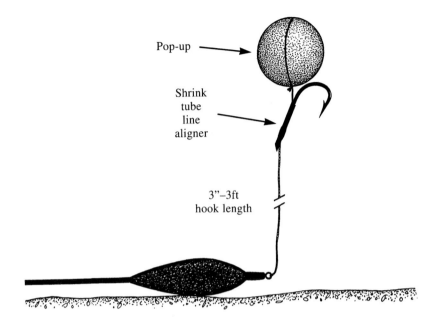

Pop-up

Shrink
tube
line
aligner

3"–3ft
hook length

Fig. 67. Pop-up off the lead

carp takes the bait into its mouth, it will almost certainly self- hook. In weed, pop the bait up so it's just above the weed stems; this is particularly effective. You would not normally use this form of presentation in a gravel pit except where the carp are cruising over shallow bars and you want a hookbait slap bang in their faces. At all times keep the hookbait tight to the hook as you want the hook to drag into the carp's mouth as soon as it takes the bait. It is best fished on a semi-fixed lead.

THE STIFFER SIDE OF THINGS

While all the presentations we've detailed are excellent in the right circumstances, they do all have one possible major failure inherent in their make up: because they all allow the hookbait to be taken in easily via the supple hooklength it can often just as easily be rejected. The supple qualities of the hooklength can work to your advantage but they can also work against you. On some waters carp will take your hookbait into their mouths time and time again but because they are fished on supple hooklinks they are rejected time and time again. However, by making your hooklength less supple, the anti-reject properties of the presentation increase and so does the likelihood of self-hooking.

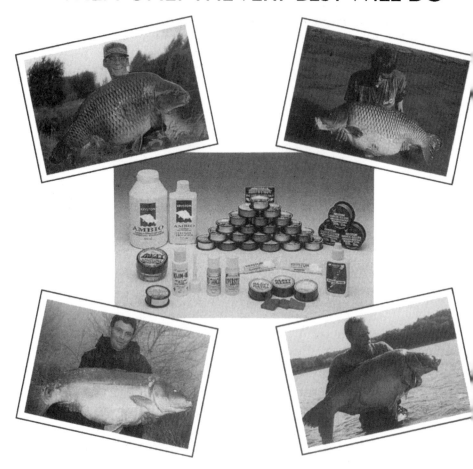

Unfortunately, it isn't possible to say which waters you should and should not use these stiff rigs on and it's all a question of experimentation. It is usually a case of, if it's not been done before (or recently) then the first to try it will succeed! They are certainly very effective in silt.

STANDARD MONOFILAMENT PRESENTATION (Fig.68)

This is the most basic of all presentations and is one in which many carp anglers have complete confidence. Normally we would advocate the use of bottom baits but a buoyant bait is useful over weed. This presentation possesses a degree of suppleness but also a better anti-reject capability than the standard hooklength. It will work well where nylon hooklengths have not been used for a long time.

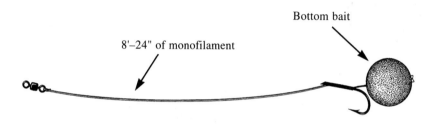

Bottom bait

8'–24" of monofilament

Fig. 68. Standard Monofilament Presentation

AMNESIA OR LEDKOR LOOP RIG (Fig.69)

Taking the stiff side of things to its conclusion we have the Amnesia loop rig. This leader is very stiff and once taken in is hard to eject. For best effect use a D-Rig on the hook, and a loop on the swivel side allows a degree of movement (Fig.70). In silt this is an excellent self hooker and by adding a stringer you increase that effect. Straight bottom baits are best on this presentation and it should be fished on a semi-fixed lead end tackle. You can even attach the hook to the hooklength via a loop. A very effective version of this rig can be made using Carp 'R' Us Ledkor for both the hooklink and hair; attach to swivel loop/hinge as shown, continue Ledkor through to hair using the no-knot system. The advantages of this is that when the carp takes the bait in, the Ledkor bends and makes ejection extremely difficult.

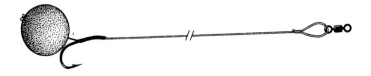

Fig. 69. Amnesia Loop Rig

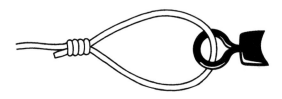

Fig. 70. Loop/Hinge

HAWSERED POP-UP (Fig. 71)

As we stated earlier, although a pop-up can be sucked in easily, once a carp seeks to reject it by blowing it out the braid will crumple up and self-hooking may be avoided. By coating the braid between hook and putty in Hawser you still have the positive effects that pop-ups have but if the carp seeks to blow the bait out the Hawsered braid cannot crumple up and instead pivots on the counterweight. This aids self hooking tremendously. You can fish this as a critically balanced pop-up but when fished overbalanced it is harder to reject. This is not a confidence presentation so use a semi-fixed lead and as short as possible a hooklength. You can also super-glue the braid instead of Hawsering it.

HAWSERED BOTTOM BAITS

You don't have to restrict the use of Hawsered braid to pop-ups as you can also make excellent anti-reject rigs for bottom baits as illustrated (Fig.72). These can be fished line aligner style or by way of standard tubing to hold the hair tight. For silt or gravel pits these are excellent presentations.

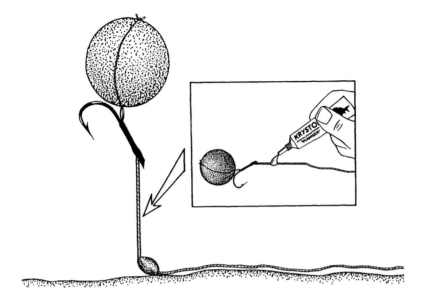

Fig. 71. Hawsered pop-up

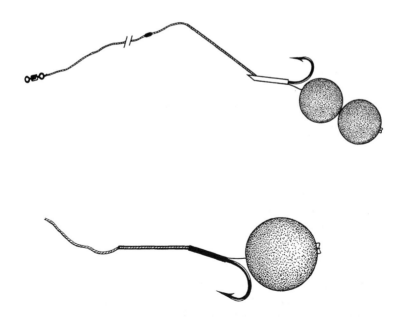

Fig. 72. Hawsered bottom baits

THE SPRING RIG (Fig. 73)

By continuing the hooklength material to make the hair, you can form what is known as a Spring Rig. You can use this kind of rig with any type of material from multistrand to stiff monofilament. However, the most effective versions incorporate either braid or standard monofilament. This spring effect is very effective indeed and works best with bottom baits. A hooklength of around 8–16 inches (20–40cm) is ideal and a straight or inturned point on the hook complements the presentation.

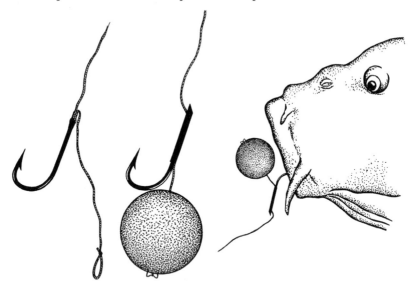

Fig. 73. Spring Rig

CONFIDENCE RIG (Fig. 74)

There will be occasions where instead of trying to get the carp to bolt, you are seeking it to pick the hookbait up and move off unhindered so that you can strike the hook into it or so that the hook catches when it slowly moves off. This is known as a confidence rig. Remember you are seeking to give the carp confidence to pick the bait up, not to cause it to bolt off!

A small light hook, such as the Partridge Z11, which was specifically designed for this rig, a fine hair and suchlike all contribute to giving the carp confidence to pick the bait up and move off naturally without bolting in panic once resistance is felt.

Although those presentations if copied should catch you carp from most waters, you should also be aware of certain considerations which relate to some or all of the presentations.

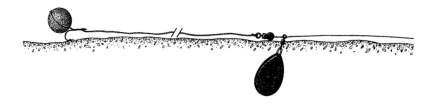

Fig. 74. Confidence Rig

a) Baits on the hook?

Although the hair rig is a very effective way of presenting a hookbait, it is not the only way and at times it can work against you. Baits can be fished on the hook with the advantage that in order for the hookbait to go into the carp's mouth so must the hook. Where carp are picking up baits this can be very effective. By mounting a boily on the hook (Fig.75) you are in effect side hooking it which will be completely different from that which is seen on most waters today. Ensure that the bait cannot slip down the hook shank or it may impede its hooking efficiency. By pushing it up onto the eye of the hook you can wedge it on which will hold it securely. After you've pushed the bait over the point and up the shank it is sometimes necessary to resharpen the hook just to make sure it's needle sharp. You can fish baits on the hook on any kind of hooklength and should vary your hooklength choice and mensions dependent on the water in question.

b) Hair Rig Use?

The purpose of a hair rig is to present a bait on a hair separate from the hook itself. Many of today's presentations involve the use of a hair rig in one form or another, so let's cover one or two of the basic considerations to look at.

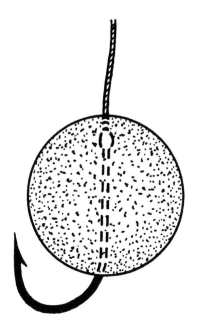

Fig. 75. Side hooking

1. Type of hair? You don't actually need to use a piece of hair (unlike KM who used his wife's hair for the first ever hair rig!), as there are plenty of viable alternatives for today's carp angler. Standard 1–3 lb monofilament makes an excellent hair but all monofilament has a degree of memory in it, so it doesn't fold back on itself quite like dental floss does. Dental floss may appear thicker than fine monofilament but because it is made up of dozens of tiny fibres which separate when wet, it will fold back on itself, thus aiding the hook finding a hold in the carp's mouth. You can also use multistrand as a hair.

2. Length of hair? The hair can be as long as you wish it to be but generally a good place to start is when the top of the bait is touching the bottom of the bend of the hook. By lengthening the hair you give the hook-bait a greater degree of free movement and make it more likely to hook inside the mouth once taken in. However, weed can find its way between hook and hair on long hairs, so impairing entry into the mouth, and you have to be careful that the hair does not tangle round the hook point. By using a shorter hair, both hook and hookbait are more likely to be taken in together but the hookbait's free movement will be decreased, and if the hookbait is rejected the hook is far more likely to follow it.

c) Buoyancy in Hooklength Materials

When you use hooklengths over 6 inches (15cm) long you will find that because most of them, apart from nylon, have a degree of inherent buoyancy you can end up with a raised loop effect between hookbait and swivel. On some waters this may make no difference at all and if you are pulling your end tackle and presentation back to a certain spot it will straighten, but on other waters it may spook the carp and cause them to ignore the hookbait, or treat it with some caution. To get round this problem you can weight the hooklength a little so that the additional weight causes the loop to be laid on the lake bed and not up in the water. This can be done in a number of ways.

1. Finger and thumb method. Put a piece of mud or dirt between your thumb and first finger and rub it up and down your hooklength (Fig.76). This deposits little particles on the hooklength which in turn causes the hooklength to be weighted and sit it down on the lake bed. You can also utilize this method by using putty in your fingers and that holds it down even better.

2. Magma'd hooklengths. An alternative method is to use Kryston's Magma liquid weight. Simply place a small blob on your hooklength every 3 inches (7.5cm) or so, allow it to dry for 60 seconds and then roll it between thumb and first finger. This will evenly coat a very small area of your hooklength in Magma and force the loop on to the lake bed (Fig.77). This is a little harder to perfect than the first one but is a little more exact in its performance.

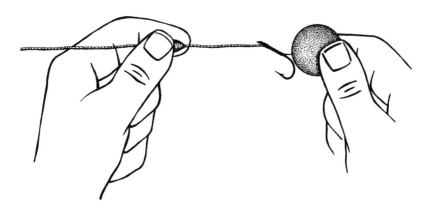

Fig. 76. Use of putty/dirt to sink hooklength

(a)

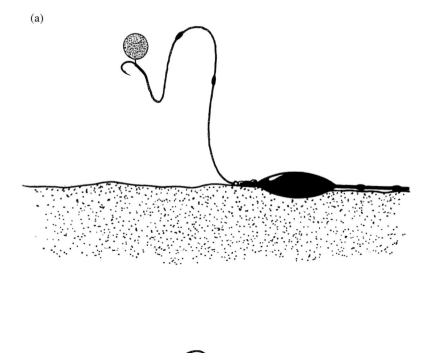

(b)

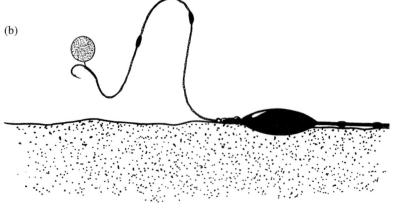

Fig. 77(a,b,c,d). Use of Magma to force down loop

(c)

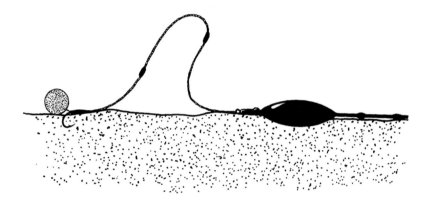

(d)

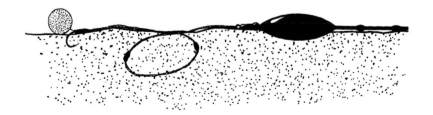

d) Length of Hooklength?

While it would be nice to be able to say exactly how long a hooklength
should be, all waters are different and, consequently, the length of a hooklength may need to be varied. Generally, on weedy waters where you are
having to use a pop-up to deal with the weed, use a hooklength which is
8–12 inches (20–30cm) including the distance the bait is popped-up.
However, don't hesitate to increase this to 20 inches (50cm) or decrease it
to 4 inches (10cm). On clear waters with standard bottom baits, use a
hooklength 5–10 inches (13–25cm) long but don't hesitate to decrease that
to 4 inches (10cm) or increase it to 20 inches (50cm). In silty waters with
very little in the way of weed or whatever, where using a bottom bait, start
at 12 inches (30cm) and decrease to 8 inches (20cm) or increase to 24
inches (60cm) to improve your chances. In short, there is no answer available but those guidelines and experience may help you.

Although at times it may be necessary to use a long hooklength this
can create problems when casting out to the required spots. Long hooklengths fly around when cast which cuts down on distance considerably.
Also, in restricted swims you may not have the room to have a long drop
when you are about to cast out. There are ways round this and you should
familiarise yourself with them (Fig.78). The first is very basic and merely
comprises folding your hooklength back on itself a number of times and
holding this firm with a wrap of PVA tape or string. The second is a little
more fiddly but is more aerodynamic for those long casts. Fold your hooklength back as in our first tactic and then coat in Kryston's Super Stiff
water soluble gel. Once it sets all the folds of braid will be held together
and will withstand the hardest of casts. However, once in the water the gel
dissolves and the hooklength is free to move to its full length.

e) How far to pop baits up?

Really there is no limit as to how far you want your pop-up to be off the
bottom, but for anything other than naive carp which haven't seen the tactic before we like the pop-up to be as near the lake bed as possible. The
higher the pop-up is off the lake bed the more visual it may well be, but as
carp can learn by association it is possible that they will eventually wise up
to baits presented too far off the lake bed (Fig.79). After all, your freebaits
will always be on or in the lake bed. For that reason, pop the bait up 1–3
inches (2.5–7.5cm) from the lake bed. This is just enough to make it easy
to locate and self-hook but not so high as to spook the carp.

f) Warning smells to the carp?

Some of the end tackles and presentations detailed involve the use of sol-
vents and adhesives such as superglue, Hawser, paint and the like. However,

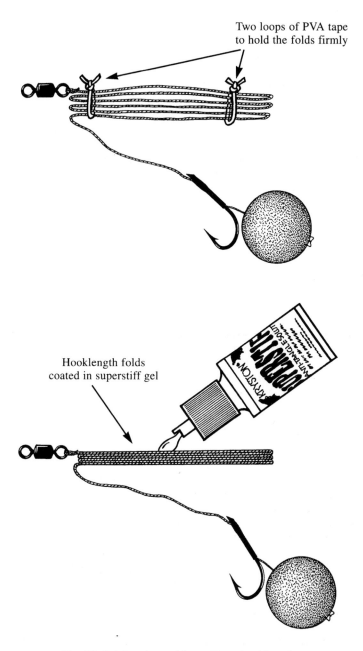

Two loops of PVA tape
to hold the folds firmly

Hooklength folds
coated in superstiff gel

Fig. 78. Solving the problem of long hooklengths

Fig. 79. Pop-up heights?

there is a school of thought that believes that the odour of these products is unattractive to carp and may cause the fish to avoid components coated with or utilising them. We have carried out test tanks to see if this is true but they do not seem to affect the captive carp at all. However, carp in fish tanks and carp on pressurised waters are totally different creatures and we cannot honestly say that this should be treated as the definitive answer; our advice is to use your common sense at all times. In theory, the smell shouldn't put the carp off but if everybody is using those products, the carp may pick up on the common denominator signal and become cautious. To the human the smell of superglue and such like is not conducive to feeding, but we are entirely different from carp. Once set, these products appear to have no discernable odour and if you follow that train of thought what's to say carp will not be wary of the smell of tubing, hooks, braid and the like? Indeed, they may be! Our advice is to use only the products you really need and use them sparingly. If results are not what they should be then start looking at this aspect.

g) Crayfish Rigs (Fig.80)

Let us be totally honest – there is no such thing as a totally crayfish-proof rig! However, it is possible to make any presentation as crayfish-proof as

Fig. 80. Crayfish Rig

possible. Crayfish are an absolute pain on many waters as they can snip the
bait off with their pincers and can nibble the hookbait to pieces. Firstly,
always use air dried baits as hookbaits as they, and some makes of readymades, are the only kind of baits able to withstand constant crayfish attention. Ensure that the boily stop is drawn into the hookbait so it can't be lev-
ered free and it is best to tie it on with at least two knots as the crayfish
somehow remove a stop which is simply pushed through a hair loop.
Recently, someone has come up with an excellent little idea where the bait
is encased in a nylon netting which allows the attractors to leak out but
keeps the bait protected from the crayfish's pincer claws. All you do is
encase the hookbait in the nylon netting and hold it tight with a superglued
knot – an excellent idea. Nylon netting is available from most general stores
or if you are stuck try using the cake covers that cake shops use to protect
their products. You can use it to cover all types of hookbaits including bottom baits, pop-ups, balanced baits etc. Whatever presentation you do decide
to use, you will need to keep recasting regularly to keep checking the bait's
still attached. Good luck!

No prizes given for identifying Kryston Heavy Metal!
The denser the putty, the better your presentation will be.

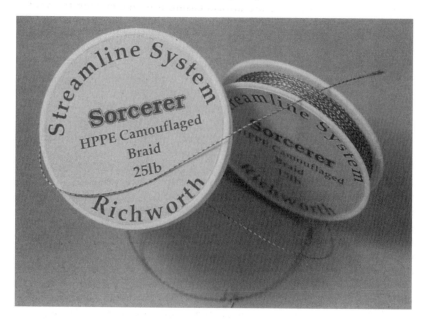

Sorcerer camouflaged HPPE braid – a very reliable hooklength material.

9. *Stalking Rigs*

Carp do visit the marginal areas on most waters and when in such areas are very catchable. By stalking carp you create another tactic to use when appropriate and it does allow you sometimes to actively select the particular carp you want to catch. You could of course use a standard end tackle and presentation but the following ideas should help. These are in addition to the end tackles and presentations detailed earlier. If you feel that the ideal rig for a particular set of circumstances is a 3 oz (90g) bomb and line aligned bait, then use it – the whole point of carp fishing is catching carp not just trying to prove a point by using float tackle etc just for the sake of it.

THE GENERAL PRINCIPLES

Whatever rig you decide to use always ensure it is fine enough to fool the carp but strong enough to land it. There will be many occasions when you can actually see carp feeding in areas which are almost impossible to land carp from, no matter what rig you use. In such cases don't fish to those spots, think about a viable alternative and pick a rig accordingly. Losing fish in weed, snags and suchlike is not clever and can put the carp's health at risk. When the carp are in catchable spots, use sensible tackle so that you land the fish. If the water's open scale down accordingly.

FLOAT FISHING IDEAS

One of the best ways to catch carp by stalking them is by way of float fishing a bait in the appropriate place. You can actually use straight through monofilament line but an effective way is to use a supple braid or multistrand between hook and float. Purchase some straight bodied wagglers, small clear river trotting floats and ensure that if they are not clear they are in colours which blend in with weed, reeds and so on. You can use a shot each side of the float to hold it in place or even better, use float rubbers (Fig.81). Unless you are fishing a bait in mid water you need to use some kind of weight to take the bait down to the bottom and hold it there. This can be as simple as a swan shot or perhaps some lead putty moulded round a stop knot or small shot. Again use a putty that matches the colour of the lake bed. You don't have to float fish baits hard on the

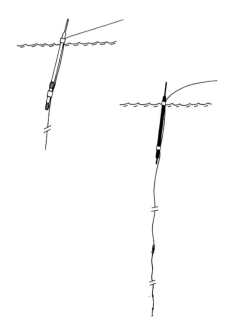

Fig. 81. Floatfishing Ideas

bottom and a very successful tactic is to use a float to present baits in mid water amongst the weed. Although this may well look crude, it is very effective.

LEGERED BAIT IDEAS

Not all waters are suitable for the float. The main stumbling block is a vertical line coming up through the swim. This is especially so on clear pressurised waters. On some waters the fish won't mind this vertical line and will happily bump into it, but on other waters they will spook if they feel or see it. For such waters you need to use a legering set-up. Although you can use a 3 oz (85g) lead in the conventional way an alternative is the one illustrated. Use a hooklength of your choice and tie it to a swivel. Behind this is a shock bead and a $\frac{1}{2}$–1 oz (15–30g) lead coated and flattened (Fig.82). This will both blend in with the lake bed and hold the bottom well despite its light weight. Of course, you don't need to use a weight and another very effective way to catch carp is by free-lining your hookbait to them. Clearly distance is a problem so it is restricted to close range stuff. However, it gives you a direct line to the carp and is the ultimate in simplicity. When the carp are close in and you can lower a bait to them it's ideal.

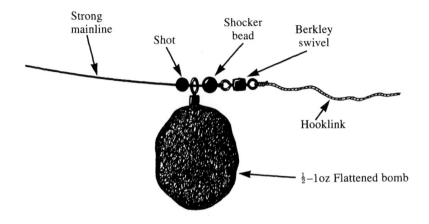

Fig. 82. Stalking set-up

Hookbait enhancers compliment a good rig when little or no free
offerings are being used, especially in winter.

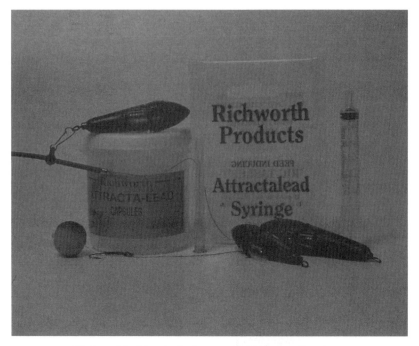

Richworth's Attracta-leads – worth trying on all waters.

PRESENTATION IDEAS

If you are using particles or boiled baits any of the ideas detailed in the book will do. From side hooked boilies to hair rigged particles they all work well and it's just a case of you using what you have most confidence in. However, if you decide to use a traditional bait like a worm, bread, maggot or otherwise, you should vary your presentation to take account of the bait's constitution. A couple of typical ideas are illustrated – keep it simple and you will catch carp (Fig.83).

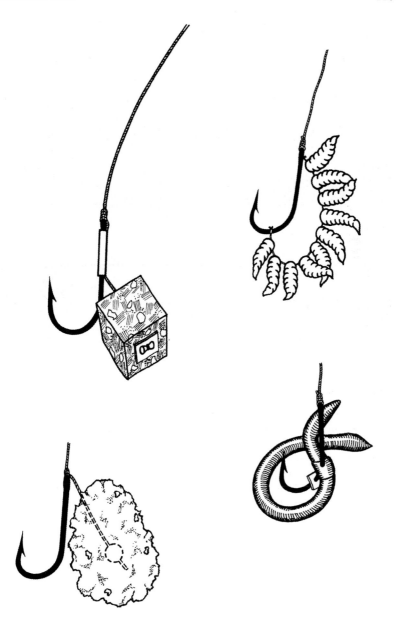

Fig. 83. Presentation Ideas

RIG PRODUCTS
from Richworth

IN-LINE LEADS

Coated in a strong & durable powder to give a camouflaged effect & longer life. Available in Green, Sand, Black or Brown.

PEAR - 1¹/₂, 2, 2¹/₂, 3, 3¹/₂ and 4 ounce
BALL - 1¹/₂, 2, 2¹/₂, 3 and 3¹/₂ ounce
BOMB - 1¹/₂, 2, 2¹/₂, 3, 3¹/₂ and 4 ounce
ATTRACTALEAD - 1¹/₂, 2, 2¹/₂, 3, 3¹/₂ and 4 ounce
ANTI-ROLL - 1¹/₂, 2, 2¹/₂, 3 and 3¹/₂ ounce
IN LINE FEEDER BOMBS - Black finish, highly effective in 1 and 2 ounce
(not including groundbait)

ALSO AVAILABLE

HELICOPTER SAFETY LEADS,
TORPEDO & BOMB - 1¹/₂, 2, 2¹/₂, 3 and 3¹/₂ ounce
ATTRACTA LEADS - 1¹/₂, 2, 2¹/₂ and 3 ounce (coated black)

   Dissolving capsules for Attractaleads, Feed inducing rig tablets, Helicopter beads, Link beads, Bufa beads, Tulip beads, Dumbell hair stops, Carp hooks (size 2, 4, 6, 8 & 10), Shrink tube, Casting boom tube, Stiff fine-bore tube, Flexible tube, PTFE tube, PVA quickmelt tubing & string, PVA bags, Tadpole rubbers, Sorcerer HPPE Braid (6, 10, 15 & 25lbs), Swivels, Baiting needles, Multi - coloured rig foam, System Hair Rigs (sizes 4 6 and 8 in 15lbs & 25lbs) and of course our famous **RICHWORTH** ready made boilie and bait ingredients.

AVAILABLE FROM ALL GOOD TACKLE SHOPS
RICHWORTH - Where Quality Counts !

10. Floater Rigs

In the last few years interest in catching carp on surface baits has rightly increased. Not all carp swim inches from the bottom, and in the right place at the right time a surface bait is deadly. The standard bolt rig may well catch a lot of carp but the thinking angler who is prepared to use surface baits will catch more carp in the long run.

As with all rigs no one floater rig will cover all eventualities and to be fully prepared to exploit certain situations you need to have a variety in your armoury. Most floater rigs are quite straightforward and follow a certain format.

THE HOOKBAIT

One thing all floater rigs have in common is that they incorporate a light-weight hookbait of one type or other. There are various types of hookbaits available so let's look at the best ways of mounting them as hookbaits.

1. Floater Cake

Although not commonly used, floater cake is an incredible surface bait for carp and is different from Chum Mixers which is essential on some hard fished waters today. Most people who fish on the surface for carp use Chum Mixers so by using floater cake you are offering carp something different which can be the difference between catching or not catching. You don't need to fish floater cake on the hair as hooking it as illustrated is acceptable (Fig.84). For full details on how to make floater cake refer to the book Carp Fever. Providing your floater cake is fairly firm it won't fall off when swirled at by carp. With these you are always sure that when the hookbait's in the carp's mouth so is the hook – now all you need to do is to strike the hook home.

2. Chum Mixers

The most popular surface bait for carp. There are many ways to present your hookbait; here are a few of the more common ones.

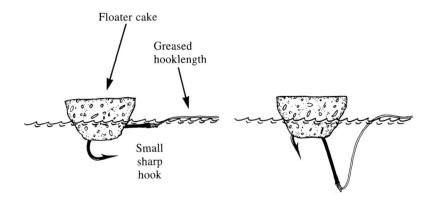

Fig. 84. Presenting floater cake

a) Bristle connection (Fig.85) – leave the spare end of your knot at around half an inch (125mm) or so, this is the retainer for your hookbait. Push your mixer over the point of the hook and carefully over the eye and past the knot. The spare end keeps the hookbait on.

b) Standard hair (Fig.86) – very simple. You can use a basic hair to hold the bait on via piercing it or you can tie the bait on with a simple overhand knot.

c) Double bait (Fig.87) – sometimes for no apparent reason the carp will prefer a double hookbait to a single one and this double hair loop is ideal for that situation.

d) Powergum/Bait Bands (Fig.88) – very fine hairs occasionally break on the cast and have a tendency to move when used regularly. By using powergum or Carp 'R' Us Bait Bands this situation will not occur and no matter how hard you cast the hookbait won't come off. The loop is superglued to the shank and will always hold the mixer in place.

e) Cork balls (Fig.89) – one of the problems with standard mixers is that once in the water they do go soggy and have a tendency to fall off. That means you have to recast which in turn can spook the carp, especially on pressured surface waters. To avoid this, you simply swop the mixer for a cork ball and it will do exactly the same job but won't fall off once cast out. Whether you fish it directly on the hook by cutting a slot and pushing the hook shank into it, or on a hair or a double bait or whatever, a cork ball duplicates a mixer almost exactly as far as most carp are concerned and they don't know it's not real until it's too late! You can add

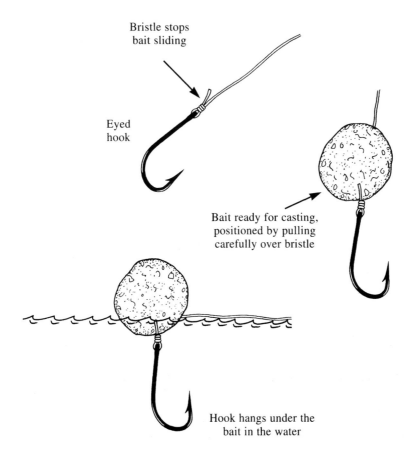

Bristle stops
bait sliding

Eyed
hook

Bait ready for casting,
positioned by pulling
carefully over bristle

Hook hangs under the
bait in the water

Fig. 85. Bristle connection

colours and flavours to them. For situations where takes are few and far between they are essential.

All the above hookbait presentations can also be used with other types of floating multiples such as trout pellets, cat and dog biscuits and so on. Whichever one you decide to use always test it in the margin to see how it sits. Sometimes you will need to slightly adjust the hair so that the hook hangs properly; this can be vital if the carp are somewhat cagey. Persevere, as you would with bottom baits, and make it work. You can use all manner of materials for hooklengths and it's a question of picking the one to match the water. On many waters standard monofilament lines such as Berkley Trilene XL are ideal but if the carp are cautious you may well have to look at a multistrand or dental floss. Always choose a hook to match the bait size and of a strength and pattern as dictated by weed, snags or otherwise. Heavy hooks have a tendancy to sink some floaters after a while so in some situations a lightweight hook is essential. The Partridge Z11 is ideal for this work providing the area is snag and weed free and you don't have to play the fish hard. A stronger version of this pattern (but still light-weight) is available under the Cassien GRS13Z name.

GETTING THE HOOKBAIT OUT THERE

Carp as we all know can be found at various ranges, from under your feet to well over 100 yards (90m) out. To present a hookbait in each situation,

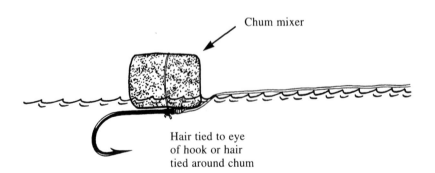

Fig. 86. Standard hair

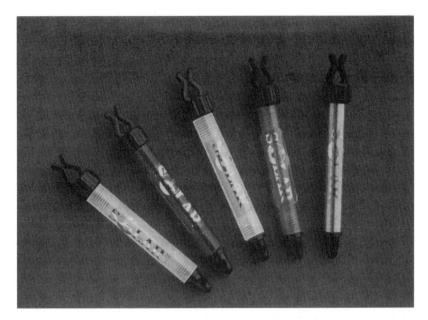

Solar's Micra-Lite-Flo's have an adjustable line clip, can take standard size isotopes yet weigh only 1 gram each!

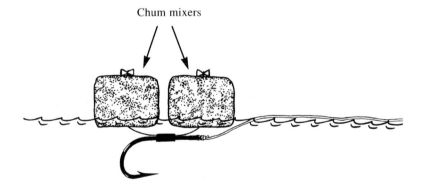

Fig. 87. Double bait

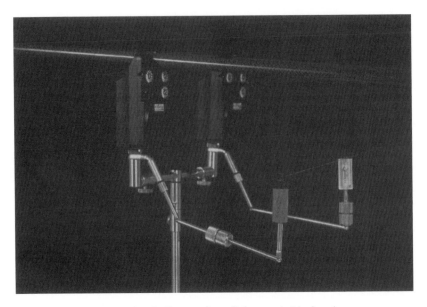

The Sensoriser Indicators from Solar – suitable for close
or long range indication.

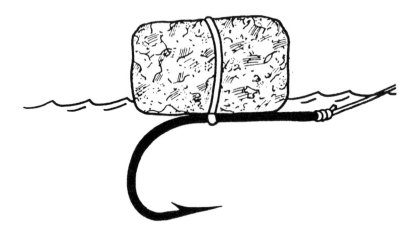

Fig. 88. Powergum or bait band loop

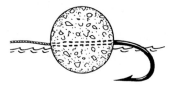

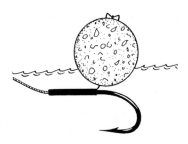

Fig. 89. Cork Ball Ideas

or at any range in between, you need to vary your end tackle accordingly. No one set-up will cover all situations so be prepared to treat each and every occasion on its own merits. Let's look at the typical situations we may find ourselves in.

1. Close Range 0–10 yards (0–9m)

If the carp are very close in, one of the best rigs to use is free-lining. No surface controllers to spook the carp and a direct line to any fish you draw the hook home into. Simply lower or flick your floater to the required spot.

Simple controller rig – using a drilled wine cork, Carp 'R' Us Iceburg or Kryston's Driftwood floating putty over the hooklength swivel you have an ideal short range set-up (Fig.90). For fishing in amongst weed and snags this is ideal and if the features are such that a tug of war is likely to occur, use Iceburg or Driftwood which will fall off the line rather than snag up. Use a sensible breaking strain of mainline and a hooklink around 12–24 inches (30–60cm) long. Your hook choice should reflect the nature of the swim in question.

2. Medium Range 10–60 yards (9–55m)

Although you can use Driftwood or Iceburg to cast a bait out up to 60 yards (55m) or so, it is far easier to use a controller which has been

THE PREPARE TO LAND
RIG MAKING KIT

FOR THOSE WISHING TO MAKE SOME OF THESE INTERESTING RIGS WE WILL SHOW YOU HOW.

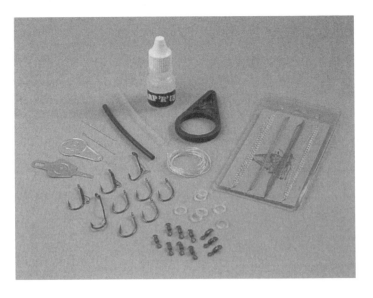

THIS RIG MAKING KIT PROVIDES THE MATERIALS AND TOOLS YOU NEED TO MAKE MANY OF THE RIGS ILLUSTRATED IN THIS BOOK.

SEE OUR RIG BOARDS AT A CARP 'R' US STOCKIST NEAR YOU.

a) Using Putty

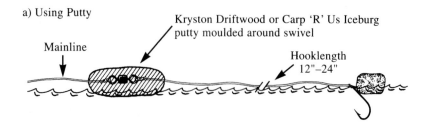

b) Using Drilled Wine Cork

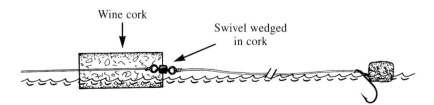

Fig. 90. Simple Controller Rig

Solar's Quiver-Loc indicator system shown here with rigid quiver tips fitted.

designed for that particular situation. For fishing at this sort of range you really need to use a small or medium sized controller. Set it up as illustrated (Fig.91) and don't cast it in until you are sure that the carp are feeding on the surface baits.

Another excellent controller rig for this sort of range is the one known as the Suspender rig. The original version was manufactured by Gardner Tackle but now a number of firms have similar or more advanced versions available. This is an ingenious device that few people use. It works on the principle of a stem made out of strong tubing about 1 foot (30cm) in length. At one end is a weight in the form of a circular tube of metal about 1½ inches (40mm) long. Just above that is a large polyball which is pierced through the centre and fixed to the stem. Your mainline is threaded up through the stem, then you join it to a short hooklink. The swivel of the hooklink is jammed into a soft rubber sleeve at the end of the stem. When you attach a bait to the hook and drop the lot into the water, the stem cocks at a 45 deg angle, so the hooklink goes down vertically with the bait and hook balanced perfectly as they just touch the water's surface. There is no line touching the surface in the immediate vicinity of the hookbait; although the stem and polyball are close by, their presence seems not to arouse the carp's suspicions. It might look ungainly, but it works well (Fig.92).

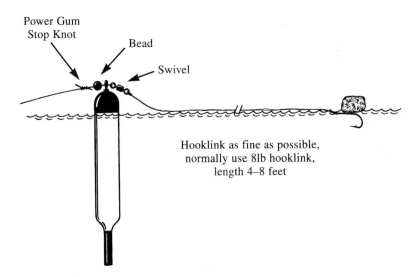

Power Gum
Stop Knot

Bead

Swivel

Hooklink as fine as possible,
normally use 8lb hooklink,
length 4–8 feet

Fig. 91. Medium Range Controller Rig

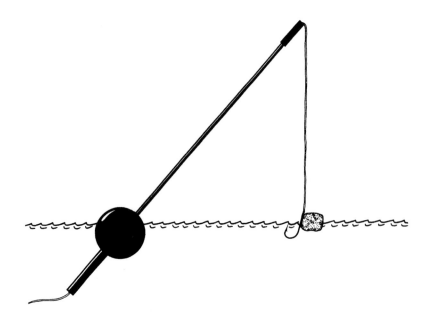

Fig. 92. The Gardner Suspender

Two tips:

  i) Grease the stem of the "suspender" as this makes it pop out of the water and not stick to the surface tension.
  ii) Make sure the hooklink is about 6 inches (15cm) as this gives the right presentation and cocks the float correctly. This controller is also a bolt rig as the swivel of the hooklink is semi-fixed inside the rubber sleeve.

Besides the advantage of no line on the water near the bait, it also has an important plus in the fact that it freely drifts around and can be used in a ripple and at range.

  3. Long Range 60–100 yards+ (55–90m+)

On larger waters or any water where the carp have been pressurised they sometimes have the tendency to feed at range and it's essential that you are able to cope with that. Yes, of course the carp may well come in closer, but by having a rig which you can cast out to that range you will always be in with more of a chance than hoping they will come closer. To start with you could use the medium range rig as illustrated and upgrade the

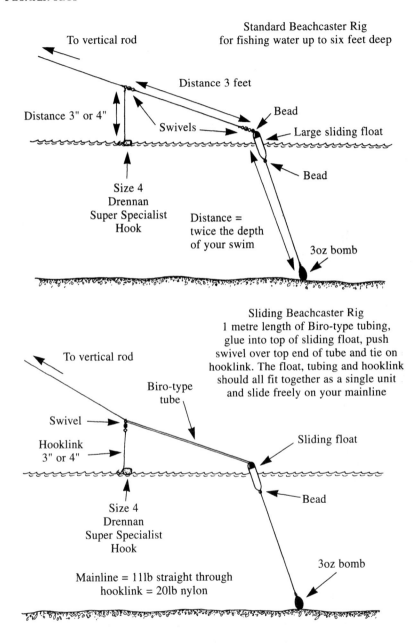

Standard Beachcaster Rig
for fishing water up to six feet deep

To vertical rod

Distance 3 feet

Bead

Distance 3" or 4"

Swivels

Large sliding float

Bead

Size 4
Drennan
Super Specialist
Hook

Distance =
twice the depth
of your swim

3oz bomb

Sliding Beachcaster Rig
1 metre length of Biro-type tubing,
glue into top of sliding float, push
swivel over top end of tube and tie on
hooklink. The float, tubing and hooklink
should all fit together as a single unit
and slide freely on your mainline

To vertical rod

Biro-type
tube

Swivel

Sliding float

Hooklink
3" or 4"

Bead

Size 4
Drennan
Super Specialist
Hook

3oz bomb

Mainline = 11lb straight through
hooklink = 20lb nylon

Fig. 93. Beachcaster Rigs

One option of three with the Solar Quiver-Loc indicator system;
stainless steel swinging arm with adjustable weight.

controller to a large controller. With a good rod and practised casting action you should be able to cast this out to that sort of range. The other version you should look at is the Beachcaster rig. As the diagram illustrates (Fig.93) you have no line on the surface and you can present a bait as far out as you can cast a three ounce (85g) bomb and accompanying floats. For rig shy carp on pressurised waters they are excellent and carp seem to take a long time to wise up to them. Obviously, they are a little fiddly to set up and can be difficult to cast – however, they are effective where the carp are wary of standard surface tactics.

11. Particle Rigs

Particles are a very effective carp bait indeed and when used on a sensible rig will account for many carp. Don't just be tempted to fish a boily over particles all the time!

END TACKLES FOR PARTICLES

Most particle rigs comprise the same two elements that standard boily rigs incorporate – an end tackle and a presentation. Later in this chapter we shall cover proven particle presentations but for now let's concentrate on the end tackle side of things. To be fair, all the previously detailed end tackles can be utilised for particle fishing. From tubed in-line rig to lead core helicopter rig all have their uses. The only ones we would advise you not to use are those which are called confidence rigs. Normally when particle fishing you are presenting a hookbait in amongst a close scattering of numerous free offerings. Because the carp does not have to move far between free offerings, there's always the danger that it may take the free offering too far back if a long hooklink and confidence end tackle are used. For that reason we advocate the use of large leads in all your presentations when fishing over beds of particles. As soon as the hooklink tightens up it needs to jar home the hook and that's where large leads work well. Always remember that the carp will be rooting round in close proximity to your end tackle so try to make it blend in with the lake bed. By all means use running leads if you are seeking early indication of the carp taking in the hookbait but fish it on a tight line and use a large lead for the reason detailed earlier.

PRESENTATION

The same principles which relate to boiled bait presentation relate to particle presentation and we won't confuse you by duplicating it. Bottom baits, pop-ups, balanced baits and such like all have their uses and it's a case of deciding which presentation should be used in which situation. All we would add is that carp can become preoccupied with particles and it's essential that your hooklength choice takes this into account. If a carp is able to take in the hookbait, and due to confidence takes it right back to the pharyngeal teeth you may find your hook link bitten off. To avoid this use a less supple hook length, don't use overlong hooklengths and, if possible, use a hooklength which is abrasion resistant. Lengthening the hair will also decrease the chances of a bite off. To aid you we include the presentations we generally use.

For larger particles such as tiger nuts and chick peas. This includes all the particles which you can thread a hair through.

a) Bottom Baits – a very simple hair rig which can be used for presenting a single particle or a number of particles (Fig.94).
b) Multiple Hair Bottom Baits – when fishing larger sized particles such as tiger nuts, chick peas, sweetcorn, peanuts and so on, it's a good idea to fish them on separate hairs as illustrated (Fig.95). Once taken, the combination of multi-hairs and a trailing hook makes it very difficult for the carp to reject the hook cleanly. A piece of cork or rig foam is used to balance out the weight of the hook. This is to be used for bottom baits only and is best used in gravel or silt.
c) Balanced Baits – using a cork ball or trimmed wine cork or rig foam you can counterbalance the weight of the hookbait, or hookbaits, so that they just sink and rest on the silt or weed. (Fig.96)
d) Pop-Ups – here the cork ball provides the buoyancy to keep the hookbait popped-up and we usually overshot the counterweight to aid with

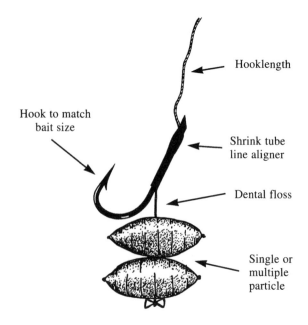

Fig. 94. Bottom bait

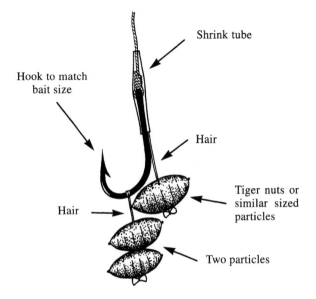

Shrink tube

Hook to match
bait size

Hair

Tiger nuts or
similar sized
particles

Hair

Two particles

Fig. 95. Multiple hair presentation

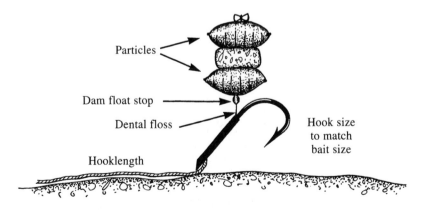

Particles

Dam float stop

Dental floss

Hook size
to match
bait size

Hooklength

Fig. 96. Balanced bait

The Carp 'R' Us Presentation, Hookum and Landing Systems boards
offer the rig-conscious angler a wide choice.

self hooking (Fig.97). With 'long' particles such as tiger nuts and peanuts you may well find they have a tendency to spin or tangle due to their shape. To avoid this mount them longways.

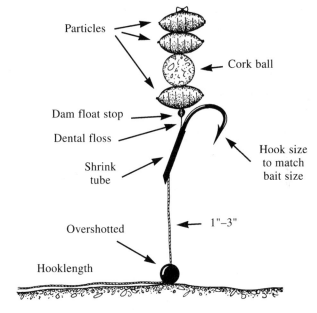

Fig. 97. Pop-Ups

e) Pop-Up Off The Lead – in dense weed or thick silt it is an idea not to use any counterweight at all and fish the popped-up particles straight from the lead (Fig.98). On a short hooklink of 2–4 inches (5–10cm) this will hook preoccupied carp.

Not all particles are big enough to fish on the hair or on the hook and with the very tiny particles called seeds you will have to use an alternative method, or methods, to present them as hookbaits. The best is by using Kryston's Bogey particle fixer which was developed specifically for this aspect of carp fishing.

PRESENTING MINI SEEDS:

a) Presenting as a Bottom Bait (Fig.99)

   1. Tie up your hook as normal and add a standard hair to it. Clip a small shot on this hair or superglue a piece of matchstick.
   2. Take a blob of Bogey fixer in your fingers and mould it round the stop so you end up with a hair-rigged piece of Bogey.

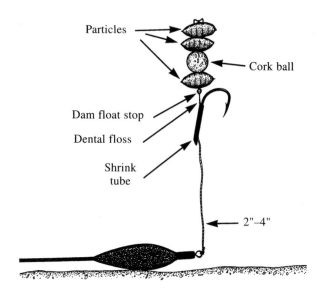

Particles

Cork ball

Dam float stop

Dental floss

Shrink tube

2"–4"

Fig. 98. Pop-Up off the lead

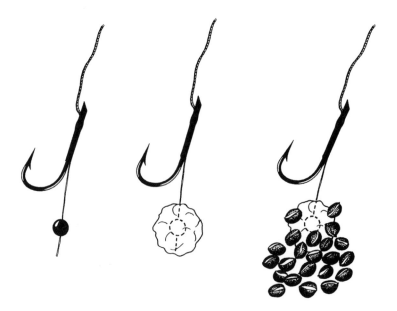

Fig. 99. Mini seeds as bottom baits

3. Dip the Bogey in your seeds ensuring they are dry, leave 20 seconds to dry and you have a presentation ready to use.

b) Presenting as a pop-up (Fig.100)

1. Tie up your hook as normal and add a hair to it. Thread the hair through a polyball and use a boily stop to keep it on.
2. Take a blob of Bogey fixer in your fingers and mould it round the pop-up as you would with paste for conventional boily pop-ups.
3. Dip the Bogey'd pop-up in those dry seeds and you will have a buoyant ball of them ready to pop-up.

As you can see from the illustration this does not look too dissimilar to a standard pop-up boily presentation (Fig.101). By adding extra weight to the counterbalance shot you can overshot the presentation or if you mould lead putty round the eye of the hook it becomes a balanced bait presentation.

Although most of the particle presentations we've detailed here are fished on standard line aligner set-ups these don't have to be and you can incorporate any of the boily presentations into your particle presentations. Big hook rig, bent hook, cranked hook, anchor rig etc – all can be adapted for use with particles and this can produce results when everyone is on

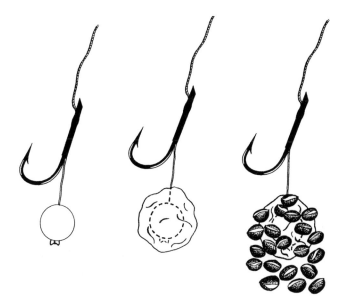

Fig. 100. Mini seeds as a pop-up

Fig. 101. Popped-up seeds

standard particle presentations. Particles fished directly on the hook can also be effective in the right situation so don't think that you have to use a hair rig – you don't! The larger particles such as tiger nuts, chick peas and suchlike can be fished on the hook and with a counterbalance of rig foam or cork you can make them almost indistinguishable from the free offerings.

12. PVA and It's Uses

Many carp anglers will have PVA in their tackle boxes but few carp anglers use the product to its potential. Yes, of course the stringer works well on most waters and PVA bags are very effective, but is it possible to use them even more effectively? For many carp anglers the answer's yes of course it is possible to make PVA work even better for you and to catch more fish. It's just one more string to your bow and with a little thought it can be an important one. PVA, or Poly Vinyl Acetate to give it its full name, has a multitude of uses and comes in a variety of guises – let's look at the important ones.

TYPES OF PVA IN COMMON USE

1. PVA Thread – available from a number of manufacturers PVA thread has a variety of uses dependent on the rig you are using. It resembles very fine dental floss and is ideal for tying back long hairs so that they don't tangle on the cast. With care thread can also be used for stringers providing your bait and hands are dry.
2. PVA String – the most common form of PVA and the one most anglers have. Lots of different companies sell this type of PVA and it has a multitude of uses from tying back rigs, stringers and so on. Dependent on which PVA string you decide to use is the dissolving time involved. The finer the string the quicker the dissolve rate – usually! Some of these PVA strings resemble thicker PVA thread and it is possible to split them to increase the rate at which they dissolve.
3. PVA Tape – not commonly used but an excellent idea which manufacturers Carp 'R' Us have made available to carp anglers. Looking like half sized Selotape or woven tape it has a fine diameter and large surface area which means it dissolves quickly. You can cut it with scissors if you so wish.
4. PVA Bags – these have been available for some time but with the popularity of PVA bagged trout pellets and the increase in weed, a number of manufacturers now sell them. Certainly Streamselect and Carp 'R' Us sell versions which have a fast dissolve rate dependent on which type you purchase. They are available in a variety of sizes and thicknesses and are extremely useful for presenting tight clumps of bait close to the hookbait.

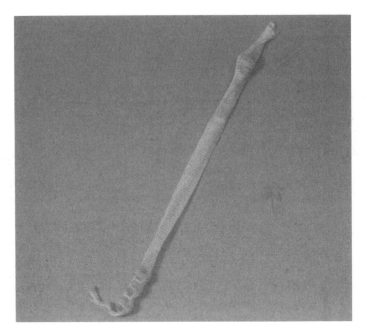

Richworth's Quickmelt PVA tubing has many uses.

A thinking carp angler should have all types of PVA in his tackle box and should experiment to find out which offers the best compromise between strength, dissolve rate and practicality.

THE GOLDEN RULE WITH PVA

When using PVA to present free offerings in close proximity to your hookbait, or even just to tie back elements of your presentation, it is vital that your PVA does dissolve. You never know when a carp will encounter your hookbait and if that hookbait is tethered or coated in PVA it will not be as effective as it could be. If the stringer is still attached to the hook it may hamper entry into the carp's mouth which can ruin your chances of a hook finding hold. The PVA brands we have detailed in the components section all dissolve so it's a case of using the PVA to maximum effect. For PVA to dissolve in water it has to come into contact with water. Knotting PVA, pulling it tight, putting baits in a tight line over it will all decrease the chances of the water being able to attack the PVA and dissolve it. In some cases it won't dissolve at all. The colder the water the more accentuated the problem is and the less effective a rig will be. So whatever type of PVA you decide to use, be aware what you want the rig to do once the PVA has dissolved. Will it dissolve the way you've used it? How long will it take

Neutral flavoured pop-ups can be sprayed, glugged
or soaked in your favourite flavour.

to dissolve? What will happen if it doesn't dissolve? Tank tests can be useful; we know all the following ideas work well providing you follow the instructions to the letter; go out and prove it to yourselves. It only takes an hour or two of your time to test all the PVA uses you are ever going to need, so take some time out to tie these up one evening.

TYING UP RIGS

If you are using a presentation which involves the use of long hairs and suchlike, there is the possibility of a tangle when you cast out. This can ruin an otherwise good rig. By retaining the hair against the shank of the hook you stop this and alleviate the possibility of a tangle. Do not tie this back with a knot or the knot will retain the hair against the hookshank. This can negate the effect of the long hair. To do this properly wrap thread round the hook and hair twice or one wrap of PVA tape once. Then using a wet finger touch the area where the PVA touches and it will seal it together similar to a heat seal on a plastic bag (Fig.102). Once cast out the thread or tape dissolves quickly and there is no knot present to hamper it. For very powerful casts or multiple bait set-ups, you may need to wrap the fine thread round three times or tape it twice – seal it with a drop of moisture.

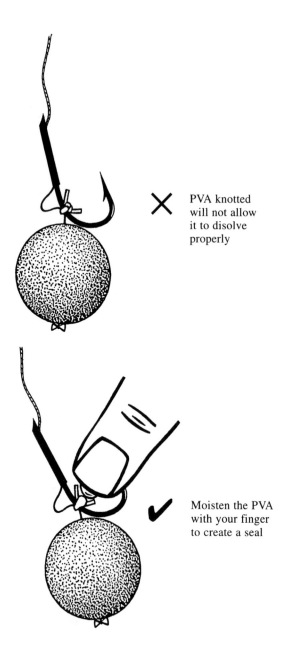

PVA knotted
will not allow
it to disolve
properly

Moisten the PVA
with your finger
to create a seal

Fig. 102. Tying-up rigs

STRINGER RIGS

In order to present a number of free offerings close to the hookbait you can use the stringer principle. Whether you are using boilies, particles or mixers, you can use the stringer method to your advantage. When you are constructing a stringer and deciding which kind of PVA to use and how to use it, remember that when it's cast out it has to withstand the force of the cast and dissolve as soon as possible. You can tie up a stringer using thread, string or tape.

a) Using thread or string

Although PVA thread and string are different in consistency when talking about stringers you can use almost the same set-ups. When most carp anglers tie up a stringer as we've illustrated it looks fine. However, once cast out the force is transmitted to the line of baits and as you can see they sometimes close up (Fig.103). Water cannot then reach the PVA so the baits end up clumped together. It may well catch carp but it does not present the free items as desired. To get round this problem there have been put forward many suggestions but the most effective by far is known as the dissolving tablet stringer rig. By putting a Streamselect dissolving flavour tablet between each bait and the hook you create the space to allow

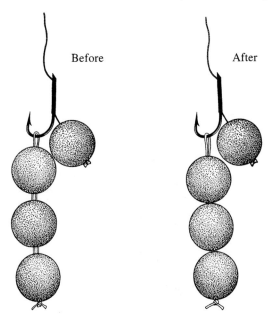

Fig. 103. Standard stringer problems

A PVA bag, complete with hook bait and free offerings, gets a final
inspection from Alan Taylor before casting.

the water to attack the PVA once the rig tablet has dissolved. This works well and will present a separate line of baits on the bottom when the tablets and PVA dissolve (Fig.104). Of course, for very short range fishing when you are using an underarm cast or lob you can use a conventional stringer but when casting with force this rig is preferable.

When casting long distances of say 60 yards (55m) or more it is inevitable that the force will be transmitted to the stringer baits and it can force the bottom stringer bait off in mid cast and allow the other baits to work free. To avoid that happening use the thread or string as illustrated and use one piece of it to go round each bait to hold it tight as illustrated (Fig.105). This way the baits will not move but will be separated when the water comes into contact with the PVA. Whichever one you decide to use, don't use a stringer needle to thread the baits onto the PVA, use a large baiting needle to drill them out a little. This will allow water to penetrate down the central hole and will aid in the dissolving of the PVA. By all means use a standard stringer needle to mount them finally.

b) By using PVA tape

Another product which is excellent to use when making up stringers is PVA tape. Because it is fine in diameter with a large surface area it is more suited to quick dissolving. Much of what is said about PVA thread or

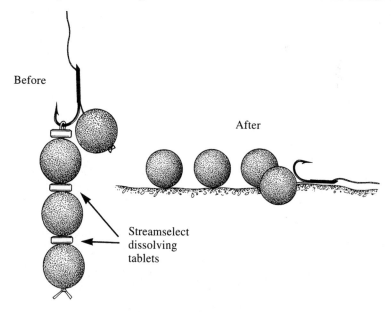

Fig. 104. Use of dissolving tablets

Fig. 105. Proper use of PVA string

string also applies to PVA tape and it's a case of amending your set-up slightly. For short range fishing where an underarm cast is used you can mount the baits as illustrated on the PVA tape and the baits will not move (Fig.106). Prick the hook point through the tape for maximum effect. For a slightly longer cast use the Streamselect dissolving rig tablets between each bait (Fig.107). This will stop them bunching up and for casts up to 60 yards is ideal. For longer range casting you cannot prick the hook point through the tape as the force will rip the tape from the hook and you will be left stringerless. In such a case, loop the PVA tape over the shank of the hook as illustrated, incorporate the dissolving rig tablets and add a small knot to retain the last bait (Fig.108). This stringer rig will resist the hardest of casts. Don't forget to drill out the central bore of the baits to aid in the PVA's dissolving.

NUMBER OF BAITS IN THE STRINGER?

Traditionally a stringer comprises three to six baits – why? There is no golden rule that you have to use that number of baits and you should not get stuck in any consistent process. Vary the number of baits and see if that improves the action you are receiving. Try single bait stringers, 10 bait stringers or whatever. Because it will be different from what most carp anglers do it may well catch the carp out and produce bonus fish for you when carp are wary of conventional stringer tactics.

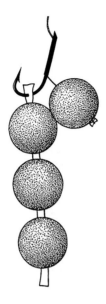

Fig. 106. Short range PVA tape use

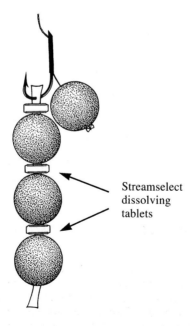

Streamselect
dissolving
tablets

Fig. 107. Long range PVA tape use

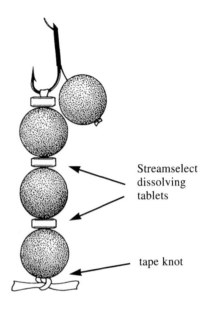

Streamselect
dissolving
tablets

tape knot

Fig. 108. Keeping the baits on

FORMATION OF THE STRINGER

Although stringers traditionally hang below the hook like a broken neck-
lace you don't have to follow fashion and it is possible to try different
ideas. Try loops of baits and see if that increases the action you are receiving (Fig.109). Why not fish a couple of separate stringers on one hook –
anything to be a little different can confuse the carp and produce takes
when the going gets tough? You could fish half baits on a stringer to
increase the attraction of the baits and you could even bait up with
stringers to accustom the carp to finding tight bunches of bait all over the
swim.

PVA BAG USE AND IDEAS (Fig. 110)

Many waters nowadays are full of weed and no matter how much you
plumb and lead about it can be almost impossible to find totally weed clear
spots. If your presentation catches in weed it can ruin it and even if the
carp could find the hookbait it is unlikely to hook itself. With PVA bags,
your confidence should be total, you know your bait is on the bottom and
not tangled in that weed. PVA bags open up whole new techniques for the
thinking carp angler, you can now fish in the weed where the carp are,
rather than trying to find totally clear spots which often the carp are wary

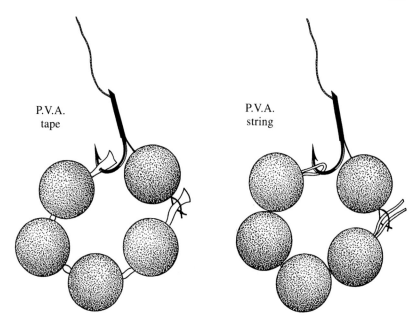

Fig. 109. Stringer Ideas

of! Even on weed free lakes they are worth trying as a different method of presentation. You have the opportunity to fish tight beds of bait round your hook. For example, a winning method on many waters is to fill a PVA bag full of sinking trout pellets, drop the hookbait into the centre of it and cast it out. This is effective on many waters. However, as many carp anglers cannot be bothered to come to grips with this style of fishing it doesn't get abused and the thinkers will succeed. PVA bags can be used in a variety of ways but the following are very effective indeed.

1. Bagging up the bait only – for short range fishing where the weed is not too bad it's often a good idea to fish your hookbait amongst a limited amount of free offerings. This can be achieved by use of a PVA bag. Ensuring that your free offerings are bone dry and so is your hookbait and presentation, pop them into a PVA bag and close the bag by using a tie of PVA string. Don't overfill the bag or it will split. Cast the rig out and once the bag hits the bottom the water will attack the PVA, dissolve it and leave your hookbait sitting in a pile of free offerings. With this you can use whole baits, half baits, chopped baits, boily crumb – the list is formidable.

2. Bagging up the whole rig – where the weed is thicker or when you want to really punch your bait out at range it is best to encompass the whole

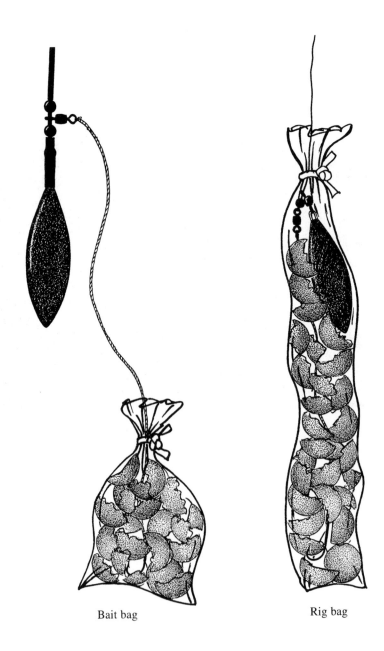

Bait bag   Rig bag

Fig. 110. PVA bags

end tackle and presentation in a PVA bag. As before ensure it's dry and also that the free offerings are. Pop it all in the bag, secure the top with PVA string, punch it out and await action.

PVA is definitely an aid in carp fishing and when used correctly it can be an advantage as well. Study the ideas we've detailed and see how those ideas can be incorporated into your fishing.

Richworth's dissolving rig tablets are available in 10 flavours
and can be very useful at times.

CARP HOOKS FOR RIGS

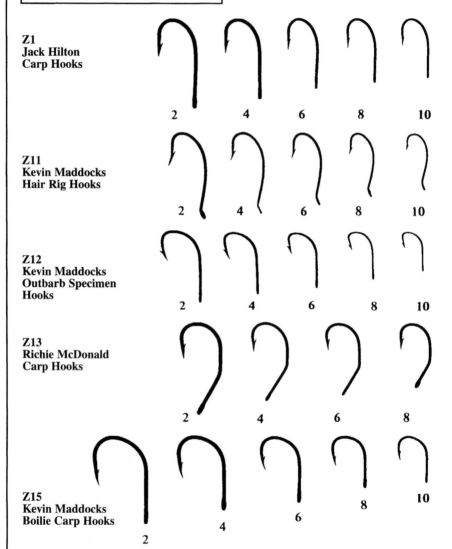

Z1
Jack Hilton
Carp Hooks

2   4   6   8   10

Z11
Kevin Maddocks
Hair Rig Hooks

2   4   6   8   10

Z12
Kevin Maddocks
Outbarb Specimen
Hooks

2   4   6   8   10

Z13
Richie McDonald
Carp Hooks

2   4   6   8

Z15
Kevin Maddocks
Boilie Carp Hooks

2   4   6   8   10

These are the hooks to be used with the various rigs described in this book.
They give you a wide range of types.

13. Water Types and Suggested Rigs

Throughout this book we've tried to detail the rigs you will need to know to catch carp from most waters today. Unfortunately, or possibly fortunately, all carp waters are slightly different and to a certain extent we can't tell you exactly what to use and how to use it. There never will be an ultimate rig to fish an ultimate way to catch unlimited fish – we hope! For that reason we have included a chapter on how to tackle six different types of waters and included for each tactics, end tackle and presentation. These are just a starting point to develop from but hopefully they will help those of you who are encountering new waters of the types listed or are struggling at your own water and need help to get those indicators moving. Whilst we are returning all fish, we are teaching them what is dangerous and as long as this continues there should never be the ultimate rig!

1. Gravel Pit

TACTICS

Visit the water as much as you can in advance and try to learn something about the water and its features. If it's visually featureless you will need to spend some time with a plumbing rod and leading rod to build up a picture of the water's topography. When at the water spend as much time as you can looking for fish before you even pick a swim. Once you've decided which swim to choose use your marker rod and your leading rod to build up a picture of what's in front of you.

END TACKLE

Once you've established the features you are going to fish to pick an end-tackle to match the situation. Usually it would be a helicopter rig but if weed is present use an in-line rig. If the water is shallow and clear don't use tubing but use a camouflaged set-up to blend in with the lake bed. Choose a lead design for maximum hooking effect bearing in mind what you are fishing on. Round leads and pear leads could produce dividends

The Alan Taylor Profile leads from Carp 'R' Us offer various
presentations including the Startle Rig.

and don't neglect the confidence rig. Lead core fly line would be a good
idea and if you are fishing at range you will need to use a shockleader.

PRESENTATION

If the water's clear be prepared to use as fine and subtle a presentation as
possible. Bottom baits are ideal and if you want an element of buoyancy
in your hookbaits use balanced hookbaits tight to the lake bed. Stringers
are an excellent idea to draw attention to the hookbait and don't forget to
stop braids looping which could spook carp. Don't neglect the stiff rig
which is very effective on gravel pits and be prepared to fine tune your
presentation as and when necessary.

2. Silty Water

TACTICS

If your water seems to be nothing but silt, silt and more silt don't despair
as the carp will still have favourite feeding spots. Even if you can't find
any underwater features by way of plumbing and leading about, you can
still find hotspots by using your eyes and ears. Watch the water as much

as you can and look for carp movement day and night. Carp head and shouldering in open water could produce a pointer as to a potential hotspot or natural food larders. Watch out for carp bubbling. Dawn and dusk are excellent times to spot carp so even if your fishing time's limited try to visit it as much as you can at these times to locate the fish. Draw a map of the water and using visual sight lines and your marker rod when necessary, mark down and locate the precise spots the carp are showing at. The hotspot may be only feet in size so accuracy is paramount. Carp will feed in most types of silt except that which is black and smells of decay. Use your leading rod to assess how deep the silt is and whether it's attractive or unattractive to carp. Normally it will hold large amounts of natural food so don't be unduly worried even if it feels deep.

END TACKLE

Unless the silt is very fine and very shallow your end tackle will inevitably be coated and hidden in it as soon as you cast out. For that reason standard in-line or helicopter rigs coupled with lead core fly line or anti-tangle tubing are ideal. By not coating your leads they will discolour easily so you can identify the type of the silt you are in.

PRESENTATION

Whilst many carp will be caught on standard supple braid presentations in silt, it's been our finding that the stiff rig is a better choice. Once the carp's taken it in, it will find it very hard to eject if it blows out mouthfuls of silt and a stringer increases the attraction of the hookbait and makes it even harder to reject. Experiment with the length of your hooklink and also the size of your hook and length of your hair. If the silt is deep you will need a longer than normal hooklink.

3. Weedy Waters

TACTICS

Don't be intimidated or frightened of weed – many anglers are and if you can approach it sensibly you can let their failures spur you on to success. If the water is heavily weeded top and bottom, you won't be able to plumb and lead all of it and it would be a far better idea to come to grips with one or two areas rather than struggle with all the water. Look for signs of fish movement or the obvious spots carp will be. Once you've decided where to fish then plumb and lead that spot thoroughly until you are totally confident that you have a working knowledge of the water in front of you. If you are not happy keep plumbing and leading until you are. On no account cast the baits into thick weed and hope. If a weedy water has a reasonable depth you will be able to feel the terminal tackle hit bottom if

These four photos show the various stages of a Carp 'R' Us
Cobweb PVA bag dissolving.

you hold your line between thumb and forefinger just before it lands. If you don't feel a slight thump, the chances are it's in weed – practice this method and there will be times when it's invaluable.

END TACKLE

For almost all weed fishing you need to use an in-line rig and a stream-lined lead. Forget the helicopter rig, in weed it is a liability. Because weed tends to grow in silt the bottom probably won't be too hard so you don't need to use round or dumpy leads which have a tendency to pick up weed. If possible try to avoid using tubing as line cuts through weed far better than tubing. Don't forget to look at using lead core fly line if appropriate and always use a sensible abrasion resistant mainline like Berkley Trilene XT in not less than 14 pounds rating.

PRESENTATION

Keep it simple and make sure it's reliable and proven. Hooks need to be strong and size 4 or 6 is as small as you want to go. Braids or monofila-ment hooklinks need to be at least 15 pounds rating and don't hesitate to go stronger if you feel you need to. Always test all your knots and don't ever risk a knot or hook if it doesn't look right. Don't overcomplicate your presentation as standard balanced baits and pop-ups work well. Don't forget the pop-up off the lead if the weed is particularly bad.

4. Snaggy Waters

TACTICS

Once you've decided which snags you are fishing to you need to establish whether such a proposition is worthwhile or not. Yes, the carp may well be in the snags and other people may well fish to those snags but can you land carp from that area? Can you land a high proportion of them – one in five is no good! Plumb around to see if you can find changes of depth close to the snaggy areas and spend some time leading about. This will allow you to feel the nature of the lake bed and most importantly will allow you to build up a picture of how far the snag extends underwater and whether there are any snags nearby which could hinder the landing of hooked fish. Be aware of how close you can cast to the snags and take account of how close you have to cast to the snags to get a take. Is that acceptable or will you lose the fish you hook? Be brutally honest with yourself and take into account the carps' welfare.

END TACKLE

Whether you decide to fish a standard bolt rig or confidence rig you must ensure your end tackle is strong enough to allow you to hit and hold the carp before it makes the sanctuary of those snags. Use a very strong proven abrasion resistant mainline such as Berkley Trilene XT and consider using a snagleader such as Kryston's Quicksilver or Amnesia if necessary. Ensure that whatever end tackle you use is not a tether rig and if the carp do make the snags and you have to pull for a break, the lead is free to come off and the carp won't be tethered in any way to the lead or to the snag. Ensure that you tailor your indication system to the end tackle you are using and always sit next to your rods so that you can strike into the carp straight away. Have a plan of action in mind and follow it through. If the snags are underwater trees, consider the fact that when using Quicksilver it is possible for a fish to become tethered and not be able to break free, thereby causing damage or possible death.

PRESENTATION

Be it a confidence rig or bolt rig your presentation needs to match your end tackle in terms of strength and reliability. Hooks need to be strong and sharp and able to withstand the initial surge as the carp seeks to make its way to the snags. Hooks that rip and tear are to be avoided at all costs. Hooklinks need to be abrasion resistant and the knots securing them to hook and swivel need to be tested. Both bottom baits and pop-ups can work well so ring the changes if no action is forthcoming. It is often worthwhile placing your free offerings away from the snags a little as this will encourage the fish to come out of the snags. If you continue to bait only inches from the snags then the carp will rarely come out.

5. Rivers

TACTICS

Location is the key for river fishing so be prepared to spend some time and effort looking for those carp. Forget all the normal rules of using plumbing rods and leading rods to find the spots, you've got to use your eyes and your commonsense. Bank walking is a must and be prepared to put the miles in to locate those carp. Also be aware that river carp tend to be quite nomadic so where they are one day may not be where they are another. Try to have your tackle with you when fish spotting so that you can take advantage of any situation that you may find yourself in. Research the whereabouts of previous catches – it might be that the carp prefer a certain area, maybe near a warm water outlet or a weedy area?

END TACKLE

Forget all the fancy end tackles you see – use basic ones. River carp do not see the carp pressure that landlocked fish see so complex rigs are not

VERY SERIOUS RODS
for
VERY SERIOUS ANGLERS

THE BLANK British made of course! Very slim and extremely lightweight. Subtle, highly attractive underlying pattern.

THE RINGS All six models feature attractive double-leg frames in shiny gunsmoke and you have the choice of gold or gunsmoke Zirconium Oxide centres - beautiful rings that compliment fabulous blanks.

THE HANDLE Unique Fuji/KM reel fitting on all Challenger™ and Exocet™ models. Custom built with extended nut and beautiful turned metal collars. Very comfortable and completely eliminates unsightly thread and the need for duplon.

THE BUTT GRIP Tough E.V.A grip in dark grey (perfectly matches reel fitting), terminated with matching turned metal collar and butt cap.

THE FINISHING TOUCHES Beautifully hand-crafted in Britain. Smooth, high gloss finish in fabulous Nightfire Red on both Exocet™ models and Chesnut Brown on four Challenger™ models. Five colour identification labels, matching steel reinforcement collars on overfit top joint, plus carbon line clip and two exclusive neoprene rod bands with all models.

THE MODELS

11¹⁄₂'	1.75lb	KM Challenger™	£230.00
12'	2.25lb	KM Challenger™	£235.00
12'	2.75lb	KM Challenger™	£240.00
12¹⁄₂'	3.00lb	KM Challenger™	£250.00
12¹⁄₂'	3.50lb	KM Exocet™	£265.00
13'	3.75lb	KM Exocet™	£275.00

These rods are available from all good specialist tackle shops. If you find difficulty in viewing one, give us a ring on the number below and we will advise you of your local stockist or arrange a no-obligation delivery to your local tackle shop. Full technical specification available free on request.

**WITHY POOL
HENLOW CAMP
BEDS, SG16 6EA
TEL: 01462 816960**

usually necessary. Providing it can hold the bottom, is tangle proof and reliable it will suffice. You may have to use up to five ounces of lead at times so use a strong mainline and sensible tackle combination. Leads need to hold the bottom under flow so choose the flat or dumpy ones and have a good supply in case you get snagged up. The Carp 'R' Us Profile leads are ideal for river fishing as they are designed to hold the bottom.

PRESENTATION

Keep it simple but sturdy. You do not need to use complex presentations and the basic bottom bait in single, double or multiple hookbait style is a proven winner. Because you could end up playing a "flow aided" carp your hook and hooklength need to be strong and as fights can often be protracted, look for a hook that winds its way in during a fight. Monofilament is an excellent hooklength and stringers a good idea to draw attention to the hookbait.

6. Canals

TACTICS

Although there is movement in the water, the carp in canals tend not to be quite so nomadic and in reality are trapped between locks. However, like river fishing you've got to locate them first and this will involve plenty of legwork and fish spotting. Once you've found the carp take note of their movements and try to establish what has attracted them to the area. If the water is featureless they may well move on, but if weed is present the carp may spend some time there. Don't go plumbing and leading about too much as you may drive the carp out and lose them. Binoculars, sunglasses and stealth are the order of the day.

END TACKLE

Unlike many river fishing end tackles you will have to be a little more subtle. Stalking fish is an excellent way to catch carp so be prepared to use light leads and float tackle. Unless you need to use tubing, avoid it, and don't use heavy leads if you are striking into the carp anyway. You won't need to use a heavy mainline unless weed and snags are present and 12 pound would be a good starting point. Beware that some canal carp are very wary so you may need to use more advanced end tackles.

PRESENTATION

Pick a presentation that matches the situation you are in. If you are fishing gin clear water tailor your presentation accordingly. Fine line, small hooks

Location proved to be equally as important as the rig for this mid-winter
canal fish of 33 pounds.

and suchlike may be necessary. However, if weed and boats are present
you will need to upgrade them to take account of that. For close range
carping you don't need to use stringers as you will almost be dropping
baits in by hand. Don't forget to try floater fishing as canal carp do fall
for this tactic on the right days.

So there you have six types of waters carp are commonly found in and
how to initially tackle that water and choose the right rig.

14. Variations for Success

Throughout this book we have detailed end tackles, presentations and tactics that are a starting point for success on many waters today. However, the ideas are a starting point only and nothing in this book should be followed with rigidity without thinking about what you are doing. All waters are different so it's impossible to say what will or will not work 100% accurately. Those are suggestions only and to be a successful carp angler on any water you may choose to fish you've got to be open minded about components, dimensions and tactics. Carp are quite contrary and frustrating at times and even on waters you feel you know you will encounter blank spells. The thinking carp anglers will adapt their tactics to counter this and will succeed; the ones who follow the same old rigs and tactics may not and may miss out. To help you in coming to terms with this facet of carp fishing we've included a number of components and tactics that can be varied to achieve different results dependent on how you vary them. Combining this section with the chapter on solving the common problems with carp rigs will hopefully produce takes for you even when others are struggling.

HOOKLENGTH

This is an area where a variation, in type or dimensions, can produce dividends especially when everyone else is using exactly the standard set-up.

a) By varying the type of hooklength used – on most waters today most carp anglers use a supple braid. Whilst at first this will produce good results and this could be for some time, supple braids are not the be all and end all of hooklengths. They do allow a great deal of free movement in that because they are so supple a hookbait attached to it can be easily sucked into the carp's mouth. Unfortunately what can be taken in easily can also be rejected easily, especially when the hooklength hasn't tightened up to the lead. By changing from a very supple braid to a more stiff form of hooklength you may catch the carp out. The inherent rigidity/stiffness in monofilament line makes it harder for the carp to reject the hookbait once it's sucked in. If it seeks to blow the bait out the rigidity of the monofilament may well force the hook sideways and so aid self hooking. By increasing the stiffness of the hooklength quite

Carp 'R' Us Ghost – the latest in a long line of nylon technology.

dramatically by use of stiff links you can take the principle to its conclusion and make it very difficult for the carp to reject the hookbait providing it has entered the mouth in the first place. You do not have to
automatically use a stiff monofilament as you could coat part of your
braid in Hawser or superglue to provide the rigidity aspect to braids.
This can be very effective indeed. Not only does the suppleness of
braids cause problems but also their touch as well. Carp will have had
braided materials across their lips time and time again and may treat
hookbaits attached to that material quite warily. By using a monofilament or multistrand hooklength you are offering the carp a different texture of hooklength. Certainly multistrand is almost undetectable when
immersed in water and the carp may well not even know it's resting
across their lips. This could cause them to take the freebait back with
confidence and draw in the hook when the hooklength tightens up
against the lead. It usually pays to be different; find out what the majority of anglers are using and then try the opposite. By copying everyone
else you can only expect to catch the same as them or less!

b) By varying the length of the chosen hooklength – whilst it's fair to say
   that most carp anglers choose to use a braid of one sort or another it's
   even more apparent that hooklengths are almost inevitably kept between
   8–12 inches (20–30cm). Don't you think the carp will wise up to this
   sooner or later -they will you know! Hooklengths do not need to always
   be around 10 inches (25cm), that's a starting point only and one the carp

may well have become aware of by now on many waters. To catch the carp out once again you could use a longer or shorter hooklink. By using a shorter hooklink of say 3–6 inches (7.5–15cm) you are cutting down on the free movement the hookbait will have due to this relatively short tether but if the hookbait and hook enter the carp's mouth, the hooklength is likely to tighten up against the lead and hopefully jar the hook home. By using a short multistrand hooklength you have an extremely supple hooklink but when the carp takes it in the hooklength does not have to move far before it jars against that lead. If you prefer to use a very stiff monofilament use the loop near the swivel to give the hookbait some free movement.

You can of course go the other way and make your hooklengths a lot longer than the standard length used by most anglers; really there is no restriction on how long your hooklength could be but 18–36 inches (45–90cm) is a good starting point. By using a longer hooklink you immediately give your hookbait a greater degree of free movement and if the carp are testing the hookbait, it will have far more "moveability" than one tethered on an 8–12 inches (20–30cm) hooklength. Also, some carp will take in hookbaits and gently move off to feel for that initial resistance in the first couple of inches. If the carp feels resistance quickly it may well seek to blow out or twist out that hook and hookbait. This they can do by spinning round or shaking their head vigorously. By allowing the carp further movement they may well think that the bait is acceptable and may move off to the next food item. Too late, the hooklength tightens against the lead and panics the carp as it has not encountered this before and you have far more chance of a self hooked carp. Do not think this happens only on pressurised waters because it happens on many waters today and you will never even know about it sitting on the bank or asleep in your bivvy. If you are catching well, obviously it is better not to alter the length of your hook link. If you are getting finicky bites, losing fish or landing them with the poorest of hookholds on the outside of the mouth, then your link needs to be a little longer. If you are getting very little action and you think the carp have been touching your hookbaits then the chances are that you will improve matters if you shorten your hooklinks.

MAINLINE

As well as being aware how a change in hooklength can work wonders, at times you should also be aware how changing your mainline can produce fish. The most obvious point is that the finer your mainline is the farther out you will be able to cast providing you use a shockleader. Clearly, you can't use very fine line in weedy or snaggy waters but by dropping down to 6–8 pound mainline your casting range will be improved tremendously. On some waters this can make an incredible difference especially if the

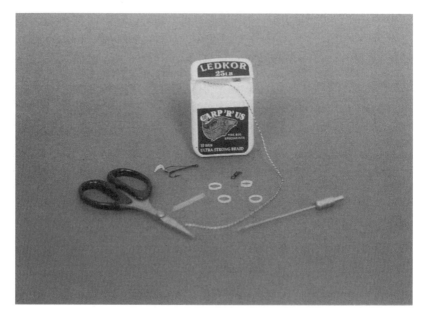

Sinks like a stone – the Carp 'R' Us Ledkor line.

carp are showing or feeding just out of range of standard tackle. Many carp anglers never use a shockleader because they can't be bothered to tie one up or haven't practised the required knot – don't fall into that trap. By adding a squirt of Kryston's "Greased Lightning" friction reducing liquid you can add even more distance to your casting range. By decreasing the diameter of your mainline you also increase its ability to transmit movement to your audible and visual indicators. In layman's terms, generally the finer your mainline is the better your indication response will be which can only be to your advantage when fish are not bolting off. Also a finer mainline is less likely to stand out in clear water conditions when it's resting across or near potential feeding areas for the carp. Standard line could spook the carp whilst a finer line may not put them on their guard so readily. Lines do vary in the cushioning effect they have when playing carp close in. Some lines such as Sylcast or Berkley Big Game are elastic so they can absorb the lunges of fish close in. Remember that stiff rods, no stretch braids and heavy leads all lead to hook pulls so some cushion effect is necessary at times. Going completely the other way, a less stretchy line such as Berkley Trilene XT or Abulon Test is ideal for fishing at longer distances when you want to be in contact with the carp straight away and don't want to have to worry about the stretch letting the carp make its way to snag or weeds. This can be vital when you need to hit and hold.

SHOCKLEADERS

By using a shockleader you can increase the distance you cast which can often be an advantage on waters where the carp feed at range, or just out of range. Shockleaders also allow you to use larger leads such as 4–5 ounce (115–145g) ones which can increase the hooking potential of some rigs. Many materials can be used for leaders and by varying the leader you can improve results at times. For standard long distance carp fishing 17–20 pound heavy monofilament will suffice but it can be a little obvious when cast over and into potential feeding areas. By using heavy braids in 25 pound rating the leader will be less obvious and should lie on the lake bed out of harm's way. By utilising a specialist leader material like Kryston's Quicksilver you can improve the abrasion resistance of the leader and also offer a sinking and camouflaged leader as well which can be an advantage when fishing in gravel pits. Don't be just tempted to use the same old leader material all the time! For achieving maximum distance keep the shockleader as short as possible – two or three turns on the spool in casting position is ideal.

LEAD CORE FLY LINE

Lead core fly line or Ledkor is an extremely useful item to use in that it sinks flat and will be absorbed into even the finest silt. By utilising this in your end tackle arrangement you can be sure that the end tackle is as inconspicuous as possible and unlikely to put a carp on its guard. There are various colours of lead core fly lines available so use one that matches your lake bed. Some are more abrasion resistant than others whilst others lie better. The big advantage of lead core fly line is that most carp anglers cannot be bothered to learn how to use it properly so if you do, you could stay one step ahead of them and the carp.

HOOK

There are dozens of different hooks available nowadays and countless different patterns. By varying the size, shape and design of the hook you can improve your ratio of pick-ups to hooked fish considerably.

a) Changing the size of the hook – generally carp are not normally scared by the look of a hook unless that hook is particularly large and the water is particularly clear. Even then the chances are that they don't know what a hook looks like. However, its size can affect your presentation in many different ways. A small hook is generally a lighter hook and a lighter hook is far less likely to be detected by a carp when it takes the bait in. Also a small hook is far more likely to enter the carp's mouth in the first place due to its dimensions. However, small hooks tend not to

Today's carp anglers have a vast array of specialist carp hooks to
choose from like these Partridge Z15's

be as strong and in protracted fights may open up or snap. By using a
larger hook of a reputable nature, it is less likely to fail. Because of their
size, once in, small hooks can very easily be rejected whilst a larger
hook, once in, has a much better chance of pricking into the carp's flesh.
However, a large hook will tend not to be as sharp as a small hook so
may not prick into flesh quite as easily. Once a hookhold is established
a large hook is more likely to hold whilst a small hook can rip the skin
due to its fine nature. The smaller your hook is, the smaller your bait
will have to be or you will find that the bait may end up bouncing the
hook out if the carp seeks to eject them. By using a large hook you can
use a larger bait or string of baits which makes rejection far harder.

b) By changing the shape/design of the hook – obviously the shape and
design of a hook has a great bearing on how effective it will be on certain waters for certain carp. As a starting point conventional straight
eyed hooks like the Ashima C-310, Drennan Super Specimen or
Partridge Z15 are ideal and account for many carp each year. However,
they will not suffice for each and every occasion in carp fishing and it's
vital to vary your hook design or shape at times. Outpoint hooks are
more likely to catch the carp's flesh when sucking and blowing is being
employed by the carp, but they have a tendency to open out or skid when
playing fish. By using an inturned point on a hook, the hook will tend to
wind its way in when you are playing the fish which decreases the

chances of the hook pulling out. However, inturned points do not find hookholds quite as easily which is a factor to take into account if the carp are testing your baits. By turning in the eye of the hook towards the point you create a line aligner situation and, once inside the mouth, as well as improving the hooking potential of the hook it tends to work the hook in when playing fish any length of time. Unfortunately, by turning in the eye of a hook, or bending the shank of a hook to create a bent hook, you are creating stress points on the hook which can cause it to fail and snap when playing carp. Always think carefully about your hook choice and weigh up the size, shape, weight, design of the hook chosen in comparison to how your carp feed, where you are fishing for them, whether they have soft or hard mouths and so on. Think, think, THINK!

HAIR RIG

Whilst you may find it hard to believe you don't automatically have to use a hair rig to catch carp. It is a convenient and often used method of bait attachment but carp on many waters have worked their way round it by now. Why not mount the hookbait on the hook for a change? That way the carp has to get the hook in its mouth if it takes in the hookbait; that alone could cause the carp to panic, bolt and set the hook. You can push baits onto the hook, side or top hook them and it will usually be completely different from what other anglers are doing. Combining a large hook, a balanced bait and side-hooking is a very effective way of catching out carp which have seen hair rigs ad nauseam. However, if you wish to use a hair rig be aware of the considerations you need to look into:-

a) Type of hairlength material – you can use various types of material to form a hair. Dental floss, fine nylon, continuing the braid, multistrands, boily bayonets etc. However, do remember that the more supple a hairlength is the more likely it is that the hook and hookbait can separate cleanly and so aid self hooking. Dental floss can be split to increase its suppleness and you can even split multistrands to make it almost undetectable. By using braids and suchlike you may well achieve a degree of anti-rejection but the hookbait's natural free movement will be restricted. Also remember that very fine hairlengths may part when cast with force or if they suffer the attentions of nuisance fish or crayfish.

b) Length of hair – most carp anglers tend to tie hair rigs that allow the hookbait to sit so it is just touching the bend of the shank. By increasing the length of the hair you increase the free movement of the hookbait and also make it more difficult for the carp to feel the hook. This is getting back to the original principles of the hair rig. Long hairs allow the hook and hookbait to separate once they enter the carp's mouth and increase the chances of the hook taking hold. Unfortunately, long hairs have a tendency to tangle if not PVA'd when cast out and if the carp are

When it's particle time get stuck in with Kryston's Bogey.
Also useful for making Heavy Metal immovable.

sucking and blowing at baits and weed is present, the hook, hair and
hookbait may get snarled up even before they enter the carp's mouth.
They may well look good in your hand but when dropped into weed it
changes.
c) Attachment of hair – whilst the line aligner is a very effective way of
attaching the hair to the hook it is constantly used on many carp waters
which will inevitably lead to it not being as effective as it once was.
Instead of using the same old line aligner that most anglers use, why not
change it a little? Have the entry and exit points changed for instance.
Instead of allowing the hooklength to enter as normal have it entering at
an angle and exiting from the side of the tubing rather than the bottom
of it. This causes the hook to turn at an unusual angle which can increase
the chance of a hookhold. Try using a very short line aligner near the eye
of the hook rather than exiting it directly in line with the eye of the hook.
Why use a line aligner at all? Try the original hair rig attachment on the
bend of the hook or next to the eye of the hook. By doing something different you are more than likely to catch the carp out!
d) Type of attachment – you don't always have to use a shrink tube line
aligner. It may well be very effective but on some waters the wary carp
have learnt that providing they don't swim away, they can manipulate
the hook out using the hardness of the shrink tube as a pivot point. By

using soft tube the carp has no fixed point to do this at and is more like-ly to work the hook in. You could whip the hair on to create a hinge effect or you could tie the spade end knot to create a line aligner effect without the need for tubing of any type. Try mounting the hair on a Drennan ring or a D-rig to aid its anti-eject properties.

TUBING

The question of how well carp can see is still debated but we think it's fairly well accepted that in shallow, clear water long lengths of dark tubing, particularly the tubing which floats, could put carp on their guard. Try dropping the use of anti-tangle tubing to see if your results improve. Often it's not the look of the tubing which is scaring the carp but the feel of it when the carp are in close proximity to your end tackle and presen-tation. Try using other methods to cut out tangles like lead core fly line, stringers and suchlike – very few people do and that anti-tangle tubing could be the common denominator that the carp associate with danger. Don't just accept that it may or may not make a difference – prove it or otherwise to your own satisfaction. Even if you feel you have to use tubing keep it as short as possible and examine all the different types that are available. Some sink, some don't – some are good and some are not. Look at the alternatives and decide which suits your water and your carp fishing situation best. Even the small bits of tubing you use on your lead, to hold your hair on etc, can make a difference. Do not be a slave to one particu-lar type – experiment and reap the rewards.

LEADS

Think about it – how many people always use a 3 ounce (85g) in-line or helicopter lead for all their fishing no matter what, where and when? By varying your lead size and design it is possible to improve results.

a) Size of lead – what are you using your lead for? Is it to jar the hook home or is it to allow you to cast out to the required feeding area? If you are using the lead to set the hook then use as large a lead as you can possibly cast to the required spot with accuracy. Yes, 3 ounces (85g) may work but would not 4 ounce (110g) pull that hook home a little deeper and make it harder for the carp to get rid of it? Perhaps even 5 ounces (140g) would be better? At the opposite end perhaps the carp have got used to the feel of resistance when the hooklength tightens up to a large lead and are carefully using it to lever that hook out? In such circumstances would it not be better to use a very light lead to catch the carp off guard? Two swan shots to half an ounce (15g) may well give the carp confidence to keep moving with the hookbait and allow you to drive that hook home.

Julian's favourite – just a few of Kryston's superb range; a specialist
hooklength for virtually every conceivable angling situation.

b) Type of lead – does it always have to be a semi-fixed in-line or helicopter rig? What about trying a running lead for a change? Would this
allow the carp to move off without being aware of the carp fishing situation it was in? Perhaps a round lead would hold the lake bed better than
a standard in-line distance one? Will the round lead roll on the gravel
and would a flat coffin type lead be better? What kind of lake bed are
you fishing on? Because of its nature will it hold all leads fairly securely anyway? What about coating the lead in the protective lead coating or
paint? Will this cut down on tangles? Is it necessary? What have you got
to lose? If you do coat your lead would it not be best to make it match
the colour of the lake bed? All this can make a big difference on many
waters.

Of course, these are not the only items you can vary to improve your
chances but they are certainly the ones which will have the most impact
when looking purely and simply at carp rigs. Look at all aspects of your
carp rig from beads to swivels, hairs to hooks and ask yourself why you
are using that particular item. Is it because of common usage or have you
chosen that item because of the particular situation you find yourself in?
Don't just follow what everybody else does – work at it!

15. Top Ten Problems Answered

Although carp fishing may very well appear to be easy at times, there will be occasions for you when things just don't seem to be going right. Fish drop off, hooks open up and the takes seem to dry up. Don't panic, it happens to us all no matter how experienced or clever we may think we are. In the chapter entitled *Variations for Success* we detail how to alter certain elements of your rigs to achieve different things whilst in this chapter we look at the common problems most carp anglers come across. Of course, there are lots more rig problems that do arise but we are sure that these ten account for many of the rig problems encountered. Look at the questions and if you too have encountered the same problems the answers provided should help you to put things right – we hope so!

Q – On the water I'm fishing the carp are rolling like mad over the baits but I'm having no luck at all. No takes, nothing! I've been baiting up for a month and the water is a standard carp lake of ten acres.

A – Although it may well be your rigs that are at fault the first thing to look at is your bait. Are you sure that the carp are eating it? Yes, of course, carp will investigate and eat almost any bait you care to put out to them but there comes a time when the carp will not take it if it is not to their liking. When you prebait you are educating the carp to picking up your hookbait with confidence. The trouble is if the carp decide they don't like the bait then all you are doing is educating them not to pick it up! Unfortunately it's not possible to say with any degree of certainty whether the carp won't eat your bait or will eat it. All waters are different and what may well turn carp on at one water may turn carp off on another. This is especially true when using a bait with strong and distinct attractors like spice, extracts and so on. Also the carp may well find the bait acceptable after its been in the water some time. When cast out the attractors or content of the bait may be too "high" for the carp to pick the bait up straight away and the carp may be waiting until it's had some time to settle out in the water somewhat. Rolling fish over a baited area suggests an initial turn on to the bait but perhaps it's a little too high in attractors for the carp to pick it up straight away. Are you sure the carp will eat that bait on your water? Have you introduced it to places where you can see it being eaten? Is it being eaten? What is the carps' reaction to it? Are they feeding strongly on it or does it seem to spook or agitate them? What about trying a similar bait with a lower attractor level in it? Perhaps start at 50% of the levels you are using and see what happens. Have you thought about using baits which have been soaked for 24 hours? Why not fish just stringers or single hookbaits to your favoured areas? Perhaps a concentration of bait is repelling not attracting the carp. Before you start to change your rigs, make sure your bait is one the carp will eat.

Q – When playing fish for no apparent reason the carp are dropping off. I'm hooking them okay I'm sure, but mid fight or sometimes when I'm netting them they fall off. What can I do?

A – Losing fish is always unacceptable but particularly so when you've played them for some time. It is not an unsolvable problem and with a little care it is possible to avoid it. Have a good look at the end tackle you are using and see if there are any obvious weak points. How big is your hook? Are you sure it's strong enough to land the carp from your water bearing in mind how long you expect to play them? If the carp are falling off then your hookhold is failing and needs looking at. Which hook pattern are you using? Would it not be best to choose a hook pattern of the inturned variety where the hook winds its way in rather than ripping out? Do you need to increase the length of your hooklength to allow the fish to take the hook further back before the hooklink tightens up to the lead and so improve the chances of a hookhold in solid flesh? If you are using barbless hooks is that the problem? How are you playing the carp and what kind of tackle are you playing the carp on? Stiff rods, line without much stretch, heavy leads and small hooks can result in hook pulls. Perhaps you need to be a little gentler when playing the fish? Can you lead it in rather than trying to bully it in? Are you keeping a constant pressure on the carp or are you dropping your rod tip too much and allowing the lead to bounce the hook out? If all these things fail, then maybe the bait is finished on your water – the carp are treating it with such suspicion that they are only ever taking it into their lips. Attend to all these factors and things should start to improve.

Q – I'm landing quite a few carp but the problem is that a high percentage seem to be foul hooked. What am I doing wrong?

A – Firstly, how confident are the carp in your bait in that water? Is it one they have confidence in or is it a bait which has been used a great deal and the carp are growing a little wary of? When carp are cautious over a bait they tend to suck and blow baits in and out to test them. This can cause the hook to find itself embedded in areas other than the carp's mouth! Perhaps a new bait would help or applying more of your current bait to improve the carps' confidence in it? What kind of rig are you using? Is it one that is used by all and sundry at the water? If so, it may be that the carp are wise to it and have found ways round it to avoid being hooked on it. Why not alter one or two of the items to make it different from the ones the carp normally come across? Longer hooklinks (16–24 inches, 40-60cm) or very short ones (2–6inches, 5–15cm) are an excellent way round that problem. If you are fishing pop-up baits are you sure that the foul hooking is not happening when the carp are in the swim feeding on the food items present? Instead of critically balancing your hookbait why not overshot it so that it can't waft about and is fairly stationary so that it can be found easier? Why not try a proven anti-eject presentation so that the carp will find difficulty ejecting the hookbait once it's taken into the mouth? Add a stringer to the hookbait to see if it makes any difference. Another possibility is that the carp want the bait but it is too strongly flavoured for them; it turns them on and they keep rolling their bodies against the bait and in amongst the baited area and occasionally foul hook themselves.

Q – I've been getting takes alright and the indicator is rising steadily and I strike into ... nothing. Am I doing something wrong?

A – Firstly, are you sure that these visual and audible indications are takes at all? Could they be line bites? Consider where your end tackle has been cast to and whether the line from your rod tip to end tackle is likely to come into contact with moving carp. Does it go over any gravel bars or through weed where a suspended line is likely to catch on the carps' flanks and give you a false indication? Is there any sign of carp movement between you and the end tackle? Are you fishing over areas where the carp may be feeding? Would a backlead cut out the chance of liners or would it be best to try a totally slack line which will lay along the lake bed? Would you be able to control a carp sufficiently on a slack line before it made the weed or snags? If it's happening very frequently, cast out with no baits on – if the runs continue then (you had a very hot curry last night!) it's definitely line bites! If you are sure it's not liners that are causing the problem then it may well be your rig that is at fault. What size of lead are you using? Is it heavy enough to pull the hook home – if not increase its size or shape for maximum effect. Is your hook sharp enough? Have you tried moving the bait closer to the hook to ensure that if the carp takes in the hookbait it will also take in the hook? Alternatively, lengthen the hook link a little as the problem might well be that the hook link is tightening up before the hook is entering the carp's mouth properly. What about fishing the bait on the hook so it has to take in the hook as well? Sidehooking can work well especially when it's been neglected. Any of these things could help.

Q – The water I am fishing is very silty and I'm not confident at all. How on earth do I place a bait on top of the silt where the carp can find it?

A – Firstly in order to decide which rig to use in silt you have to understand how carp feed and what they feed on. Lead about and find out what kind of silt you are fishing in. Unless it's the thick black smelly silt the carp will probably feed in it – yes IN IT. Carp feed where the food is and if the food items are in the silt that's where you will find the carp feed and that's where you want to present your hookbait. Certainly bloodworm and other such larvae are found in quantities in silt and these natural food larders are often the hotspots the carp feed strongest in. Even the lightest of baits will sink down into normal silt so forget about trying to use a rig which will present a free offering on top of the silt – it just isn't necessary. Your free offerings will have sunk into that silt and that's where you want your end tackle to be. Because the carp will be taking in and blowing out mouthfuls of silt along with the free offerings, you need to make your hookbait as hard as possible to eject once taken into the carp's mouth. The stiff rig is excellent in such cases and fished on a short link should hook the carp very effectively. Add a stringer to the hookbait and it makes it even harder for the carp to get rid of that mouthful. Don't be afraid of silt, once you've found the areas the carp are showing at, a carefully thought out rig should produce the required results.

Q – My local water is choked full with weed and I just don't know what to do. I'm only used to clear open gravel pits and this is completely new. Help!

A – Before you even start to worry about which rig to use make sure you can establish where the carp are, for a good bait on a good rig in the wrong place can only lead to one thing – a blank. Having sorted out where the carp are, or should be, use the feature finding techniques we detailed earlier to find the spots to place your baits. It's no use whatsoever casting your baits into the middle of weed and hoping because that's a waste of time. You may get lucky occasionally but for the majority of the time your hookbait will be snarled up in the weed and wouldn't be able to hook a carp even if the carp could find it in the first place. Use your leading and plumbing rods properly and find areas which you can actually feel your lead thump the bottom. It doesn't have to be totally clear just acceptably clear. You don't need to use fancy rigs in weed and the standard presentations will suffice. Use an end tackle such as the in-line one which won't snag in the weed when playing the fish and use proven presentations. PVA bags are an excellent idea and if they haven't been used before can produce startling results. What you must ensure is that whatever fish are hooked are landed. Use a strong mainline, a dependable hooklength and a hook which won't open up under pressure when trying to steer the carp out of the weed. And last but not least, stay with your rods at all times.

Q – The most productive areas in my local lake are next to the snags. However, I'm not sure how to approach it as some people cast right up to the snags and some well away. What do I do?

A – Unfortunately carp love to feed and lie up in snaggy areas which can be a great problem to inexperienced and experienced carp anglers alike. Whilst some carp may well frequent the snags for safety these snaggy areas often have large deposits of natural food around them for the carp to feed on. It's also a fact of life that whenever an angler fishes these spots they always bait up very close to the snags so the fish get used to finding food there and to catch the carp you sometimes have to cast very near to the snags. If that is so, you have to ensure that your tackle is up to it. Decide whether a confidence rig would be best or whether you could safely use a bolt rig. If you use a confidence rig you will have to sit with your rods to strike the hook home and if you use a bolt rig you will have to ensure that your set-up doesn't allow the carp to reach the snags before you turn it. Hooks need to be strong and proven. Your hooklength needs to be abrasion resistant and at least 15 pounds strength. Always use an in-line end tackle and if possible use one which has a weight which can fall off if necessary. Although you don't want the carp to make the snags, why not use a snag leader which will not part if the worst comes to the worst. Watch what the others are doing and see which tactic works best. Try to work out what the snags look like underwater; maybe they are undercut so that plunging your rod top into the water keeps the line low enough to avoid it snagging. How can you refine that tactic? What could you do different from them? Perhaps you could try baiting up away from the snags? Always put the carps' welfare first.

Q – I've been fishing particles and mini boilies recently and occasionally when I get a take I contact the fish briefly and then it falls off. All I'm left with is half a hooklink. What's going wrong?

A – It sounds as if you are being bitten off. When carp are feeding confidently and are in a state of preoccupation, they tend to take the free offerings and hookbait well back into their throat. This is especially true when the free offerings are all close together and the carp do not have to move far between mouthfuls. Particles and mini boilies create this situation which is both good (preoccupation) and bad (bite offs). A bite off occurs when the hooklength comes into contact with the carp's pharyngeal teeth and parts. Clearly you can't in all honesty "unpre-occupy" the carp so you have to look at the components in your rig. Make the hooklength as short as you possibly can. Most carp anglers use hooklengths of 8–12 inches (20–30cm) which may well suffice for many occasions but not for preoccupied carp. Go down to a 4–6 inch (10–15cm) hooklink and shorter if necessary. 1–3 inches (2.5 to 7.5cm) would not be too short no matter how unusual it looks. Make your hooklength as abrasion resistant as possible so lessening the chance of it parting. Because the carp are preoccupied you may not have to use subtle supple hooklengths. Thick monofilament or even Kryston's Quicksilver leader material would be a good choice. Perhaps add a frightener to the hooklength such as a piece of anti-tangle tubing. Stop that hooklength going too far back at all costs.

Q – I'm fishing for some large carp on my local syndicate lake and whilst I knew it would be hard going I feel I am not getting things quite right. All I'm getting are single bleeps and rod knocks. What do I do?

A – Firstly, have an honest appraisal of things as they stand. Are you failing or is it par for the course? What are other anglers catching? If others are catching and you are not, you definitely need to reappraise the situation. If no one else is catching you need to look at your rigs and see if you can't fine tune them a little to improve things. Although single bleeps and rod knocks could be caused by fish brushing into the line, that's unlikely unless you are fishing with your lines high in the water. Start by fishing your rods low to the ground and your rod tips close to the water's surface to keep as much line on the bottom as is possible. Try fishing a very tight line indeed with your mainline in clips to hopefully panic the carp into bolting when it feels resistance. If the rod tip's knocking and it's not down to liners your lead must be moving. Try a shorter hooklink and make the hook razor sharp and the lead as heavy as you can cast out accurately. Most importantly sit by your rods and concentrate. Set your buzzer to maximum sensitivity and strike at any movement at all if that's practicable. If you are still not connecting look carefully at the hook and hair situation. Is the carp getting the bait into its mouth properly? If so, put the bait closer to the hook and lengthen the hooklink to allow the hook to go further in. Don't accept bleeps – they could be missed chances.

Q – The gravel pit I've started to fish has got quite a lot of carp in it and although I'm catching one or two, other anglers are outfishing me. What can I do?

A – Most importantly look at how those carp anglers are fishing and compare their results, tackle, hours, experience and so on against yours. Do they have years of experience and know the water a lot better than you? What are they doing that you are not? Is it down to rigs or are they using more bait, longer hours, casting further etc? Could it be a combination of all those factors or is it just one? Bait can make a big difference as well. Are they fishing as a team and weaning the carp onto their baits? What could you do to match that? Be brutally honest with yourself and your angling. Analyse each and every factor in your fishing and see if it can be improved – you will probably find it can! Even if you are reasonably happy with the rigs you are currently using, why not try experimenting with at least one rod? If your gravel pit is shallow and/or clear, have you camouflaged your end tackle? Blend your lead, tubing, swivels and so on to match the lake bed. Are you fishing as fine as you possible could? If these carp have been caught time and time again standard carp tactics may not work so well and you may need to use small hooks down to say size 10 and light braids or fine multistrands. Drop the anti-tangle tubing, try running leads, strike at single bleeps and so on. You are half way there by noting and accepting that others are outfishing you – now go out there and do something about it.